three words

TERRY BOSGRA

Brilliant Books Literary
137 Forest Park Lane Thomasville
North Carolina 27360 USA

CONTENTS

FOREWORD;
ISSUES & EVENTS BOOK # 5

The first four books were about people who accomplished much.

This book is different; it's all topical and mostly intended for people who do not want to read large volumes about a specific issue or event. In the past I was asked to speak once or twice a year to the home-scholars about political issues in a conference room at the State Capital. Only one or two of these students came back later and asked to participate in hearings and wanted to meet legislators in their office, but the others moved on, I think this book may fill that need.

It gives the high lights of things like: The Great Wall of China, Cold War, Nicene Creed, Convention of States, Brexit, American Exceptionalism, and hundred fifty more in easy readable format. In some instances, we give you an eyewitness account which may be different from the official version. For example, my report about what happened at the *1989 Tiananmen Square Student Democracy Protest in Peking* differs greatly from the official China government report. Some years later I was sitting in a HK café enjoying my Chinese tea; there was a demonstration going on outside. I asked a participant about the meaning of the rally. She said: "*Commemoration of the peacefull protest at Tiananmen Square;*" I told her, <u>I was there</u>, <u>my friend died there, along with</u>

hundreds others, and it was not peaceful; she said emphatically no one died. I said my eyes do not lie and the tanks were not friendly. Before long, all were at my table, asking questions, telling me: One man stopped the tanks. I assured her that is a propaganda picture, varying reports say it was 19 year old Weilin Wang, referred to as Tank Man, but it could not be, and never was confirmed; world press shows pictures of the crushed bikes and bodies, reporting that hundreds died. I suggested if u want to know the truth, go outside China and search what really happened. The entire world press excoriated the China leadership for their action and shamed them before the whole world. We differ in that China hides the truth from their own people, and America airs all their dirty laundry for the whole world to see. We may never exactly know what happened but feel like the old Irish poet William Hunter when he wrote the hymn: "*I feel like traveling on*". In this book we have attempted to condense the issues or events in one or two pages while *you can be traveling on*.

ROE V WADE # 1 (500)

Today is Friday June 24, 2022 and I am writing some of these commentaries to be aired later. Like a thunderbolt, the US Supreme Court said: (what we have known for more then 50 years) there is nothing in the United States Constitution about abortion. When Justice Harry Blackman on January 22, 1973 wrote the majority rule about the Roe v Wade & Doe v Bolton case, effectively established abortion on demand up to 6 months and gave the mother (& her doctor as executioner), the right to kill her baby for a fee. Life for an unborn baby to live was legally denied and at that time the most dangerous place for a baby to live was in the mother's womb. Justice Blackman and Chief Justice Warren Burger went to the same elementary school and the same Sunday-School went fishing together, played on the same sports team. Blackmun attended Harvard Law School on the advice of his friend Warren Burger. These 2 were so close that when Blackmun wrote the majority opinion on this issue they both knew there was nothing written in the constitution, but wanted to please the feminists who had stoked up the country by such radicals as Bella Abzug, Gloria Sternum, and Bette Freidan (all 3 Jewish women), who had deep hatred for anything American. Gloria Steinem had written the book: _The truth will set you free, but first it will piss you off._ The book was pushed by Democrats and far left Republicans. In those days I was jolted me back to the days when I was raised under Hitler when pro Nazi rallies appeared all over Europe; we had learned from our parents to love our Jewish friends, even those who disagreed with us. Finally today, after almost 50 years, the justices agreed that a right to abortion had never existed in our constitution, it was simply made up, because the left wanted it. President Biden who only says what he is told to say: _the court is taking us on an extreme ideology_, but he has no idea what he is saying the left has him say what they think people want to hear. It is very sad to have a president who can not determine right or wrong but speaks what he is being told. Today's decision was no accident. We can thank president Trump for keeping his promise of appointing justices to the court who are not legislators, but as judges are doing exactly what they are committed too, and that is interpret the constitution as it is written. It is why the extreme left in America hates our constitution but prefer anarchy. Twice I have debated Mazie Hirono. Once on the Larry & Price program, and another time at the University. The students who fact checked us reported that she grossly distorted the facts, for that reason when I was asked for the 3d debate I refused and told the committee to find someone else. In spite of her many lies she is an icon in Hawaii even though she makes the dumbest comments on national media networks.

ROE V WADE NR 2 (501)

When Roe v Wade was decided on January 22, 1973, at that time I Terry Bosgra was doing my research for the book: "*Abortion the Bible & the Church*", Even for a layperson like me, it was clear that the ruling was on a collision course with the Constitution, and was done to please the far left; and a small segment of the population. Finally after 50 years the court was willing to admit that the 1973 ruling was simply made up and had no basis in the US Constitution. Do court rulings ever get reversed? *Yes* they have more then 200 times since the country was founded. Perhaps the most notorious case was Dred Scott when chief justice Roger Taney ruled that a black person was not human and should be reduced to slavery, President Lincoln battled to have that reversed but it took a civil war. This 1973 abortion ruling has been very costly. According to US health statistics after 10 years, by 1983 about 15 million babies had been killed, by that reasoning America is guilty of having executed about 75 million innocent babies, such numbers dwarf the holocaust. Not by accident but deliberate. Will God forgive America? By comparison America's historical records reveal that combat related deaths are slightly over 1 million lives. Basic Judeo-Christian principle emphasize the dignity and sanctity of human life, these principles are deeply rooted in God's Word. The right of an unborn baby to live was legally denied on the basis that a child can not live outside the womb and was not (in the language of the court), fully human. That policy of unbridled abortion throughout pregnancy has led to an alarming erosion of our society's basic Judeo-Christian principles. The ruling was re-affirmed in 1983 in a trio of opinions on challenges to abortion regulations in Missouri, Ohio, and Virginia and left no legislative door open. Even efforts to give a pregnant woman full information about her abortion decision became statutorily impossible. The only bright side was the forceful dissent of Justice Sandra O'Connor who joined the previous two dissenters of Justice Byron White and William Rehnquist (who later became Chief Justice). I have had the privilege of interviewing in person in their private chambers, Both Rehnquist & White. The abortion issue did not stay in the hospital nursery but moved to Indiana Supreme Court when a Down syndrome baby was by court order sentenced to starve to death thereby moving into the murky area of infanticide. W*hen does life begin?* According to Dr Jerome Lejuene, research professor at the university of Paris who said: *At the beginning*! I had the blessing of being the moderator at the Press interview in Boston when he said that. I thank God that the court finally reversed that horrendous erroneous decision; it is my personal opinion that perhaps 26 states will outlaw abortion or have some restriction. We will wait & see.

IS THE RIGHT TO DIE AN INALIENABLE RIGHT? (502)

The US Supreme court has decided that we have a right to live? That brought answers but raises other questions. If I have a right to live, do I have a right to die? Back in 1975, (2 years after the Roe v Wade ruling), Representative Howard Oda must have had the same thought because he introduced HB-342 in the Hawaii State Legislature which said in language we all could understand: "*Death with dignity means the painless inducement of death.*" The bill was put up for a hearing, and 14 people testified in favor including the department of health, some emphasized it was good as long as it was painless. So my question is this: "What do *you* think?" here are some other thoughts. If a right is granted to one, can it be denied to another? The law may not discriminate about a constitutional right. It may not be denied on account of incapacity or age, if it is an inalienable right it must be granted to all. What about a baby who has Down syndrome or for any other reason is not wanted, it would be for their own good. What about the elderly, especially with the huge drain on our Social Security Reserve, and the enormous medical, social and economic pressures of elderly people who are using up all the family resources or inheritance just to keep someone alive who really is devoid of the value of life. Why? Holland could be used as an example; it has been legal to die for years. Sometime ago I visited my aunty and she asked what I thought about that law. She told me this. Just before u walked in the doctor had knocked on her door with his black bag, and I told him: wrong house, it's next door. Here is what happened. Our neighbor on this street pulled us all together and said I have an illness and do not know what will happen to me but do not want to die suffering. He put his home & yard in order and this afternoon the doctor came and our neighbor will be buried next week. Could he have been cured? Or might a cure have been found? He did not want to wait. We might say if I can not be cured I want to die, my question is how? We live in an age of pleasure, rights, & wants. Now that every state can decide if a baby me be legally murdered or should live. I served for 12 years on the consulting committee of HMA to create the living will it is not a straight forward issue. The questions we struggled with during these years were such as: What is incurable? Is it Leukemia, diabetes, asthma, Quora, cancer, Polio, Ebola, baldness? I have learned to be cautious on requesting no treatmen. We must remember that the executioners of Auschwitz, Buchenwald and Dachhau were not Nazi storm troopers but were mostly medical doctors who went home to their families for lunch or dinner. If a physician will accept money for killing a baby, will he kill you with a needle when paid by your children? That's the question.

POPULATION EXPLOSION (503)

How long has it been that we have been inundated with Global Warming or Global Cooling propaganda, by the far left media, or if we go back a few more years, with Population Explosion indoctrination; when Paul Ehrlich published his book Population Bomb in 1968, we were immersed daily with headlines such as: _Food shortage worst since World War II; World Famine Imminent; 3.5 million people will die of starvation this yea_, _Battle to feed humanity is over_, and _World Food supply ends in 9 years_. Prof. Ehrlich suggested putting birth control chemicals in the water supply, and have the Federal Government licensing people allowed to have children. He proposed that families pay $600 tax on each child up to two children; increase that to $1200 for the third child. Hawaii state Senator Yoshinaga, (Who died 29 Dec. 2009), was so inspired by that idea, he introduced SB 1421 requiring women be sterilized after the birth of a 3rd child, even if she might not agree. Dr. Ted Hsia, formerly at Yale, later University of Hawaii, (referred to as the Father of Genetics), proposed mandatory sterilization of all those with defective genes. (Nazi's did that to Jewish women); Dr Hsia died in Arcadia at age 88 Feb 21 2020 in Honolulu. Liberal preachers joined the chorus, sermon titles appeared in Saturday newspapers such as: Are u hungry? If not, why not? Farmers must give all produce to food-banks; Law must mandate food be stored & distributed by food banks; Government must take control of food to save mankind. At that time we got to know Dr. Robert Sassone from Pasadena who wrote the Handbook on Population

(1970), in there he offered $1,000 reward for any valid reason why population should be limited in the next 100 years. We met 3 or 4 times a year at various National meetings on the East Coast. Last we heard: No claim was ever made for the money! Dr Jacqueline Kasun, Professor of Economics at Calif. State University stated that the world uses less then half of its available arable land, and with improved irrigation and fertilization could comfortably feed 35 billion people with an American diet. In 1974, I (Terry) served on a population panel at the University of Hawaii, when at a forum; a panelist boldly stated that in 25 years all humans in the world would only be able to live in 1 Sq foot of space. Such wild assertions made by erudite professors, are often unchallenged, as they mostly teach in their controlled world. Upon checking the facts later, we concluded if families of 4 people were given each 2 acres of land we could fit the entire world in about 5 US states in middle America. History has taught us that the schemes hatched in professional societies, (especially University Intelligentsia), have a way of creeping into the rest of society while pushed forward by the leftist media.

PROPAGANDA (504)

One of the most fundamental laws of business is repetition; it is also the most basic technique to get a message across. The more often people hear and see the same story, the more likely they are to accept the message as a simple fact. It is here that we are on risky grounds and may be prudent to listen to the great counsel from Scripture warning us to be wise as serpents and be harmless as doves; therefore to shame our free enterprise of abundance only reinforces the powers of world dictators. To apply such counsel we must encourage the elimination of state run economies and promote the free market enterprises. Most malnutrition, (outside of droughts, earthquakes, hurricanes, or floods,) is caused by governments, not by population density. Dr David Hopper, president International Developmental Research Center in Ottawa, (Passed away Nov 22, 2011 at age 84) said this: "Underdeveloped countries can feed themselves if their agriculture is modernized and their rural economies restructured; the food will have to come from their soil, their resources and their farm economies." Where antiquated farming techniques have largely remained the same for centuries, crop yields have remained low. In such countries government rulers are often dictators. In nations where farming techniques have been upgraded, crop yields have doubled, tripled, and even increased eightfold. We are not saying there is no hunger, but we are saying that nations, who experience serious hunger problems, generally are nations which are controlled to a large degree by dictatorial governments, and if they want to correct the situation it is within their power to do so. World leaders would do well to reflect why our nation's founders have chosen certain cymbals. Our national emblem is not a lion seeking to devour, or a serpent devouring its own tail, but an eagle that flies upward and onward unto God. It is the only creature on land or sea which in a time of storm will not seek refuge in a cleft, or a cave, or a rock. It soars above the storm and is a bird of great dignity and strength; the eagle has extraordinary vision which can see a fish in the ocean from a height of 3 miles. The symbol was chosen because it typifies qualities to which we as a people, and as a nation, want to aspire to be a people of dignity and strength, not just military and economic strength, but Spiritual Strength. A nation of freedom which has stamped upon its coins: "*In God We Trust*." It is a nation where Independence and self determination is valued and offers unlimited opportunity for all. America is where cultures have melted into one, leaving behind multi cultured families, but stand united as one nation where all people are equal, that's our story.

DRUGS IN OUR SCHOOLS (505)

Representative Claude Pepper promised me he would send a copy of the report as soon as the hearings were completed about Drugs in our schools, He made good and I received the 107 page report by mail and this is some of what he wrote: We are a nation suffering from a deadly disease. Our nation's youth is being decimated and slowly destroyed by a drug epidemic, Drug abuse proliferates and spread like a contagious disease and has advanced to such a degree that it menaces the health of every child in the nation today. It appears that all of us are standing around waiting for somebody to do something about it. The attack on the problem has at least 3 major facets: Legal, Medical & Educational. Each of these approaches has been a dismal failure in not having significantly reduced the extend of drug-use in the US. Prior to our school investigation everyone was concerned about it. The number of heroin addicts in our schools increased from 315,000 to 559,000 in just 2 years, this was a few years ago, do you think it has improved since that time? The committee held hearings in New York, Miami, Chicago, San Francisco, Kansas, and Los Angeles. Our preliminary examination of the matter indicated that the problem was severe, but our investigation demonstrated that the drug crisis in our schools greatly exceeded our worst expectation; all of us were repeatedly shocked by the revelations about extensive drug use in our schools. Tragically, the chances are substantial that when a parent sends his child to high school each day he is sending him to a drug filled environment; sales of all sorts of drugs regularly and persistently take place in the cafeteria, hallways, washrooms, playground, and parking lots of our schools. Sales of drugs are so prevailing that a television crew had no difficulty filming a number of heroin sales right on school property. Teenagers came from every strata of our society. Girls as well as boys handsome & beautiful in their youth have become entangled in drug abuse in their formative years while groping for maturity. Their lives are impaired and may be destroyed because we as adults failed to provide them with a drug free environment. The drug pusher is a vicious criminal to adults, but is a friend to your children. The bright side is that many youngsters just experiment but do not become more heavily involved. A small percentage has become more heavily involved and progressed from experimentation to heavy drug addiction. Students were asked why drugs? One answer was my friends do, another to escape reality. The government has provided no solution but the private sector has, Here are some: for small children *Child Evangelism*, and for high school & college: *Youth for Christ*, *Campus Crusade (Cru)*, *Intervarsity*, *Young life*, & many more.

EUROPEAN MONARCHIES (506)

In the past we have insinuated that after the demise of Queen Elizabeth, shockwaves may go through the younger generations of European Royals who are watching with bated breath as their security dissipates like a mist after the morning sunrise; all of whom have in antiquity been as secure as a baby in his mommy's lap; but now every move that the new British King makes, is reverberating through Europe, and is anticipated with fear & trembling seeing their own security evaporating like the rising sun driving out the morning mist. Monarchy was the prevalent form of government in the history of Europe throughout the Middle Ages, only occasionally competing with communism. Although Republicanism has been on the horizon for some time, it began surfacing seriously in 1918 when after the end of World War-I many nations abolished monarchies. States that gained independence after the Napoleonic wars were: Denmark, Norway, Sweden, the UK, Spain and Andorra, (*small nation between France & Spain*). Kingdoms have remained predominant, and the successors to pre-modern monarchies are: Belgium, the Netherlands, Liechtenstein, and Luxembourg. At the start of the 20th century, France, Switzerland and San Marino were the only European nations to have a republican form of government, and with the ascent of republicanism to the political mainstream, which had begun with the toppling of some kingdoms after the end of WW-1 in 1918. Although monarchies have been with us for centuries, in more recent times kingdoms have been depicted as archaic, which leaves the younger generation of European royals in waiting, (who have always had a secure future), now on shaky ground. This anti-monarchism is not new & has been percolating since the French Revolution (1789-99); Napoleon transformed the political landscape of Europe; following his defeat 1814-1815 many changes were made. Sicily and Naples were absorbed in to Sardinia to form the Kingdom of Italy. In 1918 the Habsburg rule was dissolved, a few new monarchies emerged for a brief period of time in the final years of WW-1, some being Poland (1917), Iceland, Ukraine, Yugoslavia, Lithuania, Finland, (1918) Hungary (1920), Ireland (1922) The Vatican City was recognized as a sovereign state (1929), Greece (1935), Croatia (1941), Spain 1947, & Malta (1964). Although we have not counseled too many royals, but if you are a Prince or Princess in waiting, it may be wise to prepare for an avocation other then king or queen; their future has been more promising in the past than it is today.

MORAVIAN CHURCH (507)

The Moravian church claims over one million members in the world, and are most unique, so <u>who</u> & <u>where</u> are they? The only local church, (I Terry Bosgra), have ever known was a black church while living in the Caribbean during the 1950's; and discovered they are the descendents of the <u>Sugar Plantation Slaves,</u> dating back 400 years. I love music, but could not imagine more harmonizing choirs, (even angels), while hearing them sing about a block away, and could not resist my curiosity; it being tropical, doors and windows were wide open, I walked in the church, there was no choir, no director, only an elderly man with a-three-broken-strings-guitar, who played the only string he had, and the whole church was the choir. While visiting the evening worship service I had never heard music like that. It was a black church & they sang with heart & soul praising God in perfect harmony. During my 2nd visit, near the front row, an elderly lady got so into it, she climbed on the chair and it collapsed crashing her to the floor, I thought she was dead. But the guitar man went outside and returned with a bucket of water, pored it over her and she was back on another chair singing her heart out; we never experienced such scenes in the _frozen chosen churches_, in Europe, and prompted us to do a little research discovering that the Moravians are centered in the Caribbean basin of Virgin Islands, Jamaica, Haiti, Tobago, Guyana, Honduras, Nicaragua, and others; most of these we had lived or traveled, but had no further contact with them. We already had difficulty with the Papiamento dialect, which is a mixture of Portuguese, Spanish, English, and some made up words. So where did they come from? When Czech Reformer Jan Hus was martyred and burned at the stake in Prague on 6 July 1415, his followers are the Moravians who by 1467 had their own ministry, and by 1517 the Unity of Brethren numbered about 200,000 with over 400 parishes even owned two printing presses. The 30-yr-war of 1618 to 1648, (_religious conflict primarily in Germany_), brought serious persecution, but through the patronage of Count Nicholas Ludwig von Zinzendorf, (a Noble man in Saxony), who provided a reprieve of tyranny and a new zeal to reach slaves in the Caribbean with the gospel, how? They sold themselves to slave masters who shipped them to the Plantations in West Indies, just so they could reach slaves with the gospel of Jesus. While traveling across the Atlantic they met John Wesley during a storm at sea. He went to preach the Gospel in Georgia, but was not converted yet, and was terrified the big waves might capsize the ship. He noticed the Moravian men, women, & children had no fear the ship might go down, it changed Wesley's preaching from then on. Moravians are the only people who sold their own freedom to reach slaves with the gospel of Jesus.

SHOULD AMERICA BE SAVED? (508)

Perhaps the question we should ask: Is America worth saving? If not, where do we go? Psalm 33 says "*Blessed is the nation whose God is the Lord*" In the 1950's we lived for three years in South America; there the landscape is littered with statutes and cymbals of Christ, but He is not there, the largest statue in the world is Christ standing on a 98 ft high pedestal weighing 635 metric tons at the peak of a 2300 ft mountain overlooking the city of Rio de Janeiro depicting Jesus as a symbol of Christianity, which is what it *is*, a symbol. One can not escape from the ubiquitous encounters of crosses and statutes throughout the region. The Bible says Jesus was removed from the cross, it's empty! He was crucified, died, buried, rose from the grave, and ascended into heaven till he returns. Let's look at the difference between the two America's. It may be best described by 55 men who for the most part feared God when they drafted the Declaration of Independence from England and said this in 1776: "We have staked the whole future of American civilization not upon the power of government, but upon the capacity of each and all of us to govern ourselves, according to the Ten Commandments of God." On July 4th 1821, John Quincy Adams, (our sixth President) said: "It was the highest glory of the American Revolution, beginning with leaders who were inspired by Christ. In 1931, Congress adopted the Star Spangled Banner as our national anthem, and in 1956 Congress adopted our national motto: "In God we trust," even had that stamped upon our coins. But then came 21 January 1973, when the US Supreme Court used its raw judicial power to impose an abortion law more extreme than that of any Western nation, only leaving a health exception permitting late term abortion that was so broad, a baby could be killed right up to birth. That same court, speaking for US Citizens decreed on June 24, 2022 that marriage between one man and one woman is archaic and must be redefined to include two lesbian women or two homosexual men as married couples, and be given full marriage rights as has been existing since the beginning of civilization, and now have judges there who do not know what a woman is. All of these and more, are the reason for our question: "<u>Should America be saved?</u>" As it is, our nation is on collision course with Almighty God; unless there is a national revival, America will be landing in the graveyard of failed nations. In 1741 Jonathan Edwards preached the sermon titled: "*<u>Sinners in the hands of an angry God,</u>*" (available on line), which sparked *<u>The Great Awakening</u>* five centuries ago; we likely have passed that point now, so what should be done? Rather then think: "<u>Its thee not me</u>", great revivals have always begun with <u>few</u> people earnestly pray each day: "*<u>Please God change the world, begin with me.</u>*"

SAME SEX MARRIAGE (509)

On June 24 2022, the US Supreme Court delivered a massive blow to the abortion industry when it reversed the landmark Roe v. Wade decision. The fact that the rights to abortion as expressed in Roe v. Wade was never in the constitution. It becomes obvious that this has analysts anxiously wondering now that the Trump Court seems to finally carving out some steps to get America back on track and leave in its wake the culture wars that have deeply divided the country. The most obvious place to look, experts warn, is at related rights that have been similarly under assault and that would be same-sex marriage. Marriage has been, <u>since the foundation of the world</u>, a God-ordained legal & moral covenant only between one biological man and one biological woman and there is nothing in the constitution that says otherwise; it is for that reason *that* ruling is a collision course with our constitution. Advocates for L.G.B.T.Q. rights sounded the alarm over Justice Thomas (concurring opinion overturning Roe v. Wade), calling it a potential assault on the legal doctrine protecting a wide array of other civil rights. Justice Thomas argued the court should reconsider and overturn cases guaranteeing the rights to same-sex marriage which are decided on the same basis with no grounds in the Constitution. Policy advocates and lawyers with some of the leading L.G.B.T.Q. advocacy organizations called his words a warning shot against any fundamental rights not explicitly enumerated in the constitution. When one right is taken away, every other right is at risk in our nation. Shannon Minter, the legal director for the National Center for Lesbian Rights, said the opinion put the nation "on notice". We are going to look back on this day as a turning point in the history of our nation and this is a wake up call for anyone who cares about individual freedom. To many L.G.B.T.Q. supporters these words are a call to jettison modern constitutional jurisprudence. The court has moved a lot of times in recent history to extend rights; and not to take them away, therefore this is a startling, shocking, & dangerous ruling" said Gary Buseck, a senior adviser with the Gay & Lesbian Advocates. In his opinion, Justice Thomas agreed with the majority ruling that the right to abortion was not a form of liberty protected by the due process clause of the 14th amendment and agreed with the majority ruling. When Kim Davis refused to issue a marriage license to gay couples in Kentucky, we did a commentary about that last year, Thomas & Alito issued a joint statement expressing that the religious liberty is threatened of all Americans who believe marriage to be a sacred institution between a man & a woman.

OPEN BORDERS (510)

The southern US border is wide open while most nations have closed borders. Those of us who are immigrants have not known countries with open borders, except for some in Western Europe as of recently; but still have customs officers at these crossings. We have not good memories of guards searching endlessly through cars or clothes for liquor or tobacco, during the 1950's we don't drink or smoke, and never had anything to declare. Now with open borders we drove 2 or 3 times a day through the checkpoints in Geneva, it's a plus for that area, while during the 1950's we were delayed up to 3 hours at these checkpoints and there were no fast lanes. Here is our difficulty with wide open borders in the US. It has no bi-partisan support, but is only wanted by left wing Democrats. Why? Do they have ulterior motives? The northern border is closed but not the Mexican border, while the country is flooded with Hispanics that are expected to vote Democrat. That is troubling; rather then improve our borders, it's an attempt to import more future Democrats in order to keep them in power; _that's deceptive_. While traveling with large ocean liners across the world we learned of some innovative ideas how to move people, such as: "_nothing to declare_" lanes, or "_returning citizens_" lanes, or US _passport only_ lanes. One time arriving at Honolulu airport returning from Jordon, Cairo & other Middle East nations, the passport officer said: "Aloha & Welcome Home." It was so special, I kissed the ground. Here are our concerns about the open border crisis: For several years Democrats have been in control, but have not governed the country wisely, making it difficult to hold power. Subsequently large numbers are leaving the Party, resulting in self inflicted losses. It's a plus to have less paperwork and skip interminable inspections, making crossings more comfortable, simplify immigration and less hassle when visiting family back & forth, who live in border town on both sides; However times change and the downside, for open borders is: easy for criminals, drug cartels love it, import too many unskilled workers by-passing highly qualified labor, unskilled labor not assimilating, sending money to families in home countries with no sense of belonging, no efforts to learn culture or language. Home is not here but the country of birth. Open borders is a divider, not a unifier. We would support it if voted upon by Congress and agreed by both parties. We do not support the subversive and unscrupulous way it's done by left wing Democrats now, while 1.7 million, have entered illegally just in one year, (of whom we have no medical or criminal history), that is destructive; legal immigration is good for any nation if supported by the population and their representatives.

SCOPES TRIAL (511)

Can you explain to me the Scopes trial? The response I got prompts this commentary. It was a legal case of: _The State of Tennessee_ v. _John T. Scopes_ commonly referred to as the _Scopes Monkey Trial_ held in July 1925. What was the issue? John Scopes a high school teacher was accused of violating Tennessee's Butler Act which made it unlawful to teach human evolution in any state-funded-school. The trial was held & deliberately staged (in order to attract publicity), to the small town of Dayton Tennessee. Scopes was unsure whether he had actually taught evolution, but he incriminated himself deliberately so the case could have a defendant. Scopes was found guilty, and was fined $100, ($1,500 in today's money), but the verdict was overturned on a technicality. The trial received intense national publicity as reporters from all over the country flocked to Dayton to cover the high profile lawyers who had agreed to represent each side. William Jennings Bryan, three time presidential candidate & former Secretary of State, argued for the prosecution, while Clarence Darrow, (an agnostic) served as defense attorney for Scopes; the Modernists said evolution was not inconsistent with the religious teachings of the Bible, but the Fundamentalists argued the Word of God, as revealed in the Bible, takes priority over human knowledge. The case was seen as a theological contest and the trial was about whether evolution should be taught in schools. John W. Butler a farmer, and head of the World Christian Fundamentalists Association, lobbied State Legislatures to pass anti-evolution laws. He had some success, and the law was passed in Tennessee, although he later stated: "I didn't know anything about evolution… I'd read in the paper that children came home from school & told their parents the Bible was all nonsense." The trial was in response to the ACLU who had financed Scopes. Judge John Raulston accelerated the convening of the grand jury to indict Scopes despite the meager evidence against him. Scopes was arrested but never actually detained. Paul Patterson, owner of the Baltimore Sun put up the $500 bail. The original prosecutors were friends of Scopes, and were eventually replaced. The trial was covered by journalists from around the world. When the judge quoted from Genesis he was accused of being biased. Ay the 7th day the judge took the unorthodox step and called atty. Bryan to the stand, and due to the heat, as well as the overcrowded courtroom, he moved the proceedings to the front-lawn outside. After hours of heated arguments the defense made a final attempt for closing arguments but the judge had enough of it, and denied only to have the jury come to a guilty verdict. At that time the majority of Christians denounced evolution. There is much more but this is the synopsis of it.

DUTCH FARMERS PROTEST (512)

Dutch *boerenprotest*s were triggered by a government proposal to limit agricultural pollution in the Netherlands by reducing the countries livestock. The protesting farmers are motivated by a lack of respect for what they do. Having been born on the farming area and lived later in The Hague (the seat of government) I say amen to the farmers. The Netherlands is the 2nd largest agricultural produce exporter in the world, after the US. Climate activists have become more common in the government and formed the Green Party; the social liberal idealists mandated that farmers transition into sustainable farming, but have no understanding of the physical labor and long hours that farmers work subsequently these two ideologists are on a collision course. Having lived in both sides, the divide is of mammoth portion and not easily healed. One study indicated that cow dung is responsible for the damaging effect of the high nitrogen in the soil thus accusing the farmers as the key polluters. The farmers formed what could be called a union so they could protest in unison. Farmer Bart Kemp said politicians lack the intelligence of farmers and claimed that the protests were the biggest ever undertaken by farmers. Agriculture minister Schouten said in speech farmers must reduce their livestock by 50%; but the farmers turned their back on her & drowned her out. Since the legislation protests have sprung up in all 12 provinces; in some they stormed the government building. In Den Haag the military was called in but farmers had organized and done their homework. They organized rallies, blockades of busy highways, in Apeldoorn there was a jailbreak to free protesters. In Heerenveen farmers blocked roads with their tractors and the police deployed teargas. In Groningen a road was blocked with tractors till 6 pm people could not move north or south the entire day. In Friesland some fisherman began blockading ports in solidarity with farmers. In Parliament chambers angry voices were heard. Some farmers dumped large truck loads of manure in major highways. Dutch & European courts have ordered the Dutch government to deal with it & solve the controversy; some border crossings were completely blocked with hundreds of tractors; where things got totally out of hand, the police fired warning shots at the protestors. Lawmakers have given farmers till 2030 to reduce their livestock by 30 to 50 %. The farmers point out that 54,000 agricultural businesses exported 95 billion Euros in 2019 making the country of 17 million inhabitants a food superpower. The Dutch government was given the choice between food security and climate change they chose the latter. The overwhelming sympathy is with the farmers. The elites react the same as those in Canada. The Dutch people do not want to destroy their farms to save the planet; which makes about 0.46 % of the worlds CO_2 emissions.

NUREMBERG TRIALS (513)

Beginning Nov.1945 the most notorious tribunal was held against the top ranking masterminds of World War-II. Nazi Germany had inflicted the worlds most heinous atrocities ever committed on human beings. From 1939 to 1945 they waged war on Europe, invading Poland, Yugoslavia, Norway, Denmark, Netherlands, Greece, Soviet Union, and others, accompanied by immense brutality in occupied areas with systematic murders primarily aimed at Jews. The victims (*just in the Soviet Union*), included 27 million dead, in addition to the thousands in concentration camps such as Dachhau, Auschwitz, & Buchenwald, being the most notorious ones, as well as 500 brothels where sex slaves were housed to service soldiers; pregnancy was routinely routed to gas chambers. People in these camps were systematically starved, abused or subjected to medical experiments, where sedatives were not employed. It became evident that war crimes had been committed requiring an international court, to assemble irrefutable evidence, with purpose to convict & educate about atrocities the level never seen before; this required competent legal professionals, who employed hundreds of social-science researchers, such as translators, psychologists, interpreters, resulting in multiple charges. The US chief prosecutor was Supreme Court Justice Robert H. Jackson. The trial was to be for retribution as well as being educational, with the US, Great Britain & France being the key players. The work of drafting the indictments was divided: The British worked on the aggressive war charge; the French & Soviets were assigned to crimes against humanity; and the US delegation outlined the overall Nazi conspiracy and criminality. Adolph Hitler & Joseph Goebbels had committed suicide and could not be tried; Eichmann escaped to Argentina under assumed identity but was later caught, tried, convicted & hung in Israel, his final statement amounted to: _"I obeyed orders."_ All Nazis were allowed counsel of their choice. During the trial, as the evidence was presented all, (including some of the Nazis), were repeatedly shocked. One had said: I'm going to lunch with my family, route "_the pigs in the mass showers_", but wait till I get on the roof to the glass window, then release the gas slowly; I don't want them to die fast, but suffer slowly while suffocating & gasp for breath. 19 miles of film, 25,000 photographs, & 110,000 documents were presented. All defendants were top Nazi's but denied personal involvement, only gave orders, most pointed to: "_Hitler made me do it_". 12 were sentenced to death, 10 were hanged, 3 received a life sentence; all are dead now. Evidence of guilt was overwhelming; one surprised Nazi asked the court: "_How did it come to this?_" To which the judge responded: "_It came to that when u first condemned innocent life._" Is that a message for us today about abortion?

PARTY PLATFORMS (514)

Upon our arrival in America we were advised to join and support a political party that would line up with our principles. Therefore, rather then tell u how to vote, we have researched what each party is currently espousing and has publicly stated where they want the country to go. We have discovered that the majority of people do not know what their party stands for not because of ignorance but it's not an issue that is too much in the minds of voters. There was a time that the differences were minor issues between the parties, that is no longer so. Here are 6 issues that might influence your thinking: **Abortion** _Democrats_: Abortion must be accessible to all; right up to the moment of birth, it is core of who we are, and crisis pregnancy centers around the entire country need to be shut down. _Republicans_: Life begins at conception and unborn children have a right to live, the big issue is not whether it's a baby, science has clearly established that. The issue now is the location of the child. **Same Sex Marriage** _Democrats_: men marry men, and women marry women is a civil right, and should be permissible as established by the US Supreme Court. _Republicans_ Laws must protect marriage between one man & one woman which has been so from the moment God created us centuries ago; Children need a father & a mother, it's good for society as a whole. **Religious Liberty**: _Democrats:_ Health & Human services require medical providers to provide gender transition services even if they have religious or conscience objections. _Republicans_. America's health care professionals should never be compelled to choose between following their faith, and practicing their profession, religious liberty is a sacred right. **Gender**: *Democrats* introduced the transgender bill of rights embracing sexual orientation to include transition services and must ban so called "conversion therapy." *Republicans* God created man & women differently; it's an undeniable biological fact. **Education/Parental Rights**: *Democrats* will protect rights of children who want transgender surgery, and exclude the parents. In the classroom children belong to the school; parents who do not agree should be considered domestic terrorists. *Republicans*: Parents are the child's first educators, and have a right to direct their child's education. Who knows what is better for children than mom or dad? **Federal Spending**: *Democrats*: forgive $440-$600 Billion student loan. Federal spending 2021-2022 highest in US history. *Republicans* Forgive student loans is a slap in the face to working Americans who sacrificed to pay their debt; advocate caps on spending and accelerate repayment of what is now owed. (Questions, call the station, who will direct the call to us).

BOSTON TEA PARTY (515)

The Boston Tea Party was an act of protest about the fact that American Colonies were required to pay taxes on tea they had imported, and to make matters worse, the tax would not benefit the colonies but was to prop up the failing well-connected competitor: _East India Company_. The controversy was the contentious Tea Act of 10 May, 1773 which was the final spark that ignited the revolutionary movement in Boston, in addition to the fact that these were the people who for the most part had left Britain over the issue of high taxes, and the fact that a British Company had been granted favorable advantages over colonial tea importers. The Boston Tea Party Leaders were British Americans who fiercely objected to the high taxes imposed by the king, and had left Britain mostly for that reason; as well as the fact that the colonies had no representative in Parliament. New York & Philadelphia had already turned the tea ships back to Britain, but the Royal Governor of Boston held them in port, where the issue came to a boiling point on 16 December 1773 when "_The Sons of Liberty_," disguised as American Indians, came on board and threw the chests of tea into the Boston Harbor thereby destroying the entire shipment. The British government considered the protest an act of treason and responded harshly. The colonist had disconnected their roots in the fatherland, and were pioneers attempting to survive in the New World, we know that alone is not easy. Some had participated before in the prevention of unloading tea in three other areas but failed to do so in Boston because the governor had strong commitments to London, which was exactly what the pioneering colonists wanted to get away from. After the Boston episode the controversy escalated into the _American Revolution_ which became an iconic event in US history inspiring the colonists who were determined to create an America that was very different from Britain. In 1775 Parliament passed a Conciliatory Resolution to end taxation; it did not appease the colonists and in 1778 Britain made a second attempt, that also failed. John Adams, (2nd US President), and others, opined that tea drinking was unpatriotic and Americans turned to drinking more coffee. That may be the reason about the fact that coffee shops are as hard to find in London, as it is trying to find tea rooms in America. There have been political Tea Party movements in the US, (we were involved in one). It was more about non functioning elected office holders who only secured their seat wanting to stay till retirement. We believe it's better to elect successful business people; they serve one or two terms and go back to their career.

PUBLIC CORRUPTION &
CIVIL RIGHTS (516)

When on 16 June 2015 candidate Donald Trump cane down the golden escalator in the New York Trump Tower, and announced that he would be planning to run for the highest office in the land, the Department of Justice saw a business man coming to the Washington Elite and that would be a major threat. It is a fact that in order to win a campaign for the office of president is an expensive endeavor, and much of the money generally comes with substantial strings attached, politicians are told, if elected what will be expected of them. The problem here is that Trump is a self made business man with a successful track-record, and did not need dark money in order to get on the ticket he could finance most of the funds that was required. For the Washington Elite this set off major alarm bells and before the escalator reached the ground floor a multimillion-dollar leftist battle plan was set in motion beginning with a smear campaign accusing him that the Russians were behind Trump. A massive enquiry was mobilized and the justice department appointed FBI agent Robert Mueller who was mandated to produce the fact that Trump was financed with dark money from Russia, and prove that he was guilty. The entire country was exposed for 675 days while more then 500 witnesses were interviewed and $34 million later there was no proof of wrong doing, but that was no longer an issue. Trump's opponent Hillary Clinton had concocted the Russia Hoax, fabricated a phony dossier and proof or no proof it did not matter; <u>Trump was a Russian spy</u>. In the meantime the American people did not want Hillary Clinton and elected Donald Trump as president of the United States who began on day one to clean up the entire Washington bureaucracy beginning with the department of justice, and the media, but the corruption was much deeper. At one time America had a media who would say: <u>not so fast, prove your point, or you will be exposed to the real truth</u>. But now the Media, the Democratic Party, and the Justice Department are all the same entity, therefore who will be held accountable? Unfortunately there is no one; and since Trump might expose the entire left, "*Come Hell or High Water,*" he, and all his associates must be kept out of US leadership position, even if nothing ever get proven, the Trump name, must be fatally damaged imperiled, and an anti Trump campaign must be so well coordinated and activated, so that he and all his Associates must be indicted on "*trumped up charges,*" guilt or innocence, will not be an issue, even if the charges are false, the Democratic-Party-Media will repeat it often enough that the masses will believe it making all Trump associates unelectable for some time. This is the new America, and we challenge any one to prove us wrong. Just think: *How did we get here?* Perhaps it's called mass hysteria.

LEADERSHIP (517)

On the topic of leadership, we realize that Lana is presenting, but much of this is very personal and has been key to our success. Three California Companies trained me in leadership, all attempts failed and after four years we returned to New Zealand; a year later came back and settled in Hawaii, again tried the financial world; this time with my new mentor Joel, 10 yrs younger. Other trainers said: _Do as I tell u_, but Joel was different, he said: "In one week I will take you to lunch, please make a list what you want me to do to help u build a successful financial business, and I will do it, _that is leadership_ and with his coaching over 45 yrs, we developed a very prosperous small businesses with 8,000+ clients which became the envy of the industry. Here is some of what we learned; **1**. Take responsibility for our own failures, including restitution for damage we caused, make no excuses; **2**: Adapt to the clients needs, listen to them and find why they are here, how will our product be beneficial to this customer; **3**: Confidence in the product that we bring to market, if we sell it, will we buy it for our family? And follow through to see if promises are kept, ensure satisfaction; **4**: Focus on, and support team workers, recognize and appreciate their qualities, meaning the client is _not always_ right, be sensitive to staff needs, share financial success with those who made it happen, allow them to make an error, no one is perfect, correct staff in private, never in public; **5**: communicate in clear language, make sure the client understands what we tell them about meeting their need; **6**: Solve problems quickly, do not wait till later; **7**: respect others, even if not agree always show respect and treat people with dignity; **8**: Stay current on new developments, take advantage of educational opportunities, attend seminars; **9**: Prioritize personal development, make sure the staff is current on new products, take time for self improvement. **10**: withdraw to a quiet place for strategic thinking, plan for tomorrow dream the impossible dream; **11**: Keep office in presentable condition, make sure people like to come there and enjoy a warm and relaxed atmosphere; **12**: Always speak the truth, never promise what we know we can not do. A client calls for me, when I am busy, never allow staff to say *He's not in,* when I am in. instead say: He is with someone can I help u, or, when & where can he call you back. Leaders are not born nor inherit titles. Most are self made; they take charge, lead, and inspire followers. Leaders are <u>readers</u> they <u>learn</u>, and <u>ask questions</u>: keep an open mind, and motivate others, stumbling blocks become stepping stones; adversities are opportunities, when given a lemon, make lemonade. Real leaders display <u>empathy and support</u> for those who struggle, they don't say *Follow me,* people already are.

PRAYER IN SCHOOL (518)

Steven Engel (a parent), sued William Vitale (President of the School Board) in New Hyde Park NY; objecting to the prayer cited each morning by the school children at the beginning of the day even though it was voluntary. The case was carried forward by the ACLU and traveled from one court to the next till it reached the US Supreme Court who decided in 1962 <u>it is unconstitutional to have a State Sponsored Prayer.</u> On the other hand students are free to pray in public schools <u>alone</u> or in <u>groups</u> as long as it doesn't disrupts or interfere with the rights of others. In 1962 that school prayer was labeled as dangerous, therefore we should take a look at it and decide if we agree or disagree. This is the prayer, which was student led and not required. Here it is: "<u>*Almighty God, we acknowledge our dependence on Thee and we beg Thy blessings upon us, our parents, our teachers and our country*</u> <u>Amen</u>" We are not advising you whether or not this was dangerous, you decide that. But we do believe it was in general a good idea for children to acknowledge their dependence on our Creator; we are not certain if the prayer was a <u>general rule,</u> or a <u>mandate</u>, or <u>a state law</u> in 1962. The critics, who may have argued for or against, are at least both right in this: <u>Gone are the days when one faith, (historically Protestant Christianity, for the most part dominated the public schools and the public square), and much of the social ills since that time have been linked to the absence of prayer in the school house.</u> The drug issues, school shootings, and general respect for authority, can not be correlated to the fact that the children no longer begin each day with a school honored prayer. Some of it may have contributed to the general deterioration of the classroom atmosphere, but lets start by stating the obvious, it may be difficult to pinpoint one specific culprit, although we believe there is a great deal of truth to the fact that God is not permitted pretty much anywhere else in America. He is not honored in many homes, therefore would not be honored in the lives of the average teacher either. A 15 yr old boy came up with a school prayer, here are some of his lines: "*Now sit me down in school, where praying is against the rule; our hair can be purple orange or green; it's not offensive it's a freedom scene; the law is specific and precise, Prayers spoken aloud are a serious vice. We're allowed to cuss and dress like freaks, and pierce our noses, tongues, and cheeks. Ten Commandments are not allowed, no Word of God must reach a crowd. It's illegal to teach right from wrong, such judgments do not belong. It's scary I must confess, when God is not here, it's a mess, Amen.*" This boy lives in Winnipeg and was given an A for this essay.

ECUMENICAL CREEDS (519)

In the first centuries after the Apostles were all gone, the church fathers realized that the writings of the Bible could be stated in few words such as a creed, which resulted in: <u>The Apostles Creed;</u> it's not called that because the apostles wrote it, they did not! It is called that because it's a brief summary of their teachings, setting forth the doctrine in solemn, inspiring way in amazing unsurpassable brevity in beautiful order and with liturgical solemnity as written in early century understanding of Christendom. As small children our parents taught us to memorize it; that was not difficult because it was recited during the Sunday-afternoon worship service; and in the morning worship an elder would read *The Ten Commandments*. We do not know why most churches have abandoned the practice, although the Catholic and Episcopalian churches still recite them. Perhaps it is one of the reasons so many churches have drifted far left. This is not an indictment, but we are just stating a fact that today the average person in the pew does not know what the doctrinal statement of their church is. In its present form, more than other creeds, The <u>Apostles Creed</u> is often justly called the Ecumenical symbol of the Christian faith, written in 12 simple statements called the <u>Apostles creed</u>; here it is: "*1. I believe in God the Father, Almighty, Maker of heaven and earth. 2. And in Jesus Christ, His only begotten Son, our Lord; 3. He was conceived by the Holy Spirit, born of the virgin Mary; 4. Suffered under Pontius Pilate; was crucified, dead, and buried, He descended into hell; 5. The third day*

He rose again from the dead; **6.** *He ascended into heaven, and sitteth at the right hand of God the Father Almighty;* **7.** *From thence he shall come to judge the living and the dead;* **8.** *I believe in the Holy Spirit;* **9.** *I believe a Holy Catholic Church, the communion of saints;* **10.** *The forgiveness of sins;* **11.** *The resurrection of the body;* **12.** *And the life everlasting. Amen".* Unfortunately many Protestants have had difficulty with item 9 *a Holy Catholic Church.* In the 1ˢᵗ Century there was no <u>*Roman*</u> Catholic Church; the statement simply refers to universal Christianity as the early church fathers understood the church was to be established according to the Scriptures. We understand that opinions vary about the use of creeds during Worship Services, but do believe after speaking in many Protestant Churches here in the Islands, as well as the mainland and Alaska, over a period of more then 50 years, it could be beneficial to read the Ten Commandments from the pulpit, or together as people of God recite the Apostles Creed. Only one time a young man (while coming in the church) said: Welcome back, I remember you speaking here before, I said: <u>*"Thank u, what do you remember about me?"*</u> He said you are the <u>"Jehovah's Witness</u> speaker". That did not make us feel any better.

NICENE CREED (520)

The Nicene Creed is a statement of the orthodox faith that dates before the Council of Nicea in 325 AD and before the Council of Constantinople in 381 AD; although neither of them drafted it but the early Christian church did accept it. There was always a need for the creeds. As far back as the days of the apostles there have been heresies in the church and then, as well as today, the creeds define truth, correct error, and outline standards of rules for God's people. It teaches the church how to worship and confess the faith of the church fathers; it summarizes the faith and defines Christian unity. As soon as the Apostles were gone, false teachers came in and spread many heresies in the churches, Timothy had to deal with Hymenaeus and Philetus who were a gangrene on the church, the early church fathers struggled with Arianism, (named after a priest in Alexandria of Egypt who was a teacher in the first century, and taught that Jesus was begotten by God the Father, but was a creature distinct from the Father and subordinate to him). Such heresies agitated the church up to the fourth century especially as it concerned the doctrine of the Trinity and the person of Christ. The Greek, the Eastern, the Latin, or the Western church held the Nicean creed in honor from the first century till now. The creed expressed the general belief although it was erroneously held for many years that these councils had drafted and designed it. They did not! But accurately reflect the beliefs and teachings of the church fathers; here it is: "*I believe in one God, the father Almighty, maker of heaven and earth, and of all things visible and invisible. And in one Lord Jesus* *Christ, the only begotten Son of God, begotten of the Father before all* *worlds; God of God, Light of Light, very God of very God, begotten* *not made, being of one substance with the Father, by whom all things* *were made. Who for us men and for our salvation, came down from* *heaven, and was incarnate by the Holy Spirit of the virgin Mary,* *and was made man, and was crucified also for us under Pontius* *Pilate; He suffered and was buried and the third day He rose again* *according to the Scriptures; and ascended into heaven and sitteth on* *the right hand of the Father; and He shall come again, with glory,* *to judge the living and the dead whose kingdom shall have no end.* *And I believe in the Holy Spirit, the Lord and Giver of life; who* *proceedeth from the Father and the Son who with the Father and the* *Son together is worshipped and glorified; who spake by the prophets.* *And I believe one holy catholic and apostolic church. I acknowledge* *one baptism for the remission of sins; and I look for the resurrection* *of the dead, and the life of the world to come. Amen".* We point out that Protestant <u>and</u> Catholic churches have honored the Nicean Creed, as well as the Apostles Creed and the Athanasian Creed.

HEIDELBERG CATECHISM (521)

Prince Frederick III charged Zacharias Ursinus, Professor at the Heidelberg University in Germany <u>and</u> Caspar Olevianus to compose a new Catechism intended as a tool for teaching young people to be a guide for preaching in the provincial churches, and a form of confessional unity among the several protestant factions in the region, Even though Prince Frederick was Roman Catholic, he wanted Calvinism to gain ascendancy in his realm. Reformation was getting a strong foothold throughout Europe and Calvinism to gaining grounds and was rapidly spreading all over Germany and in much of Europe. The project of formulating such a task required the work of a team of ministers and university theologians working together. Ursinus served as the primary writer and Olevianus had a lesser role. As a team they generated what is now known as the Heidelberg Catechism, produced within the walls of the oldest University founded in 1386 on the banks of the river Neckar, where the entire area became a city of literature. The university was a scientific hub, of internationally renowned research facilities including the European Molecular Biology Laboratory. The request of Prince Frederick was a major undertaking but after a long arduous process by a team of learned men working in harmony the Heidelberg Catechism was born and first published in 1563 consisting of 129 questions & answers divided in 52 sections, one for each week, a genius way to formulate a statement of faith. The Catechism has been beneficial for young & old. I Terry Bosgra was one of the recipients; our parents taught us to memorize one of the sections every week and recite it before mom who insisted we do it with proper emphasis on the right issues. Mom was ill in bed but we could not fool her as she had already memorized most of the 129 question & answers. The entire Catechism was a concise and sufficient guide from the whole Bible beginning with question one: "_What is your only comfort in life and death?_ Answer: _That I with body & soul, both in life and death am not my own, but belong unto my faithful Savior Jesus Christ; who with His precious blood has fully satisfied for all my sins; and delivered me from the power of the devil; and so preserve me that without the will of my heavenly father not a hair can fall from my head; yea, that all things must be subservient to my salvation, wherefore by His Holy Spirit, He also assures me of eternal life, and makes me heartily willing and ready, henceforth to live unto Him._" The catechism helps us discover how powerful the gospel really is and how <u>wide</u> and <u>long</u> and <u>high</u> and <u>deep</u> is the love of Christ.

COUNCIL OF TRENT (522)

Let's look at the Council of Trent. You may ask where is Trent or why a council? Trent is a picturesque, historical, scientific, educational, and financial center in Tyrol which is a district in Northern Italy and we may have some insight why Calvary Chapel, and the Southern Baptists were not invited to attend the Council meeting and why did the emperor call for the meeting? Here is the answer; they only wanted Roman Catholic Bishops, Cardinals and Catholic people of learning all of whom were in attendance at the 19th ecumenical council that was bringing the most important members of the Roman Catholic Church together. The meeting was not continuous but began on 13 December 1545 and ended 18 years later on 4 Dec. 1563. The purpose was to respond to the Protestant Reformation and re-define authentic Catholic Doctrine regarding some of the following issues such as: Salvation, the Sale of indulgences, the Sacraments and react to the teachings of Martin Luther, and the entire Protestant movement which was getting out of control and spreading like cockroaches when the light comes on. Unless something was done rather quickly the Pope and the Cardinals might need to seek unemployment. The council struggled with these issues which had created so much confusion that the Roman Catholic Church was facing serious loss of dominance in the communities; therefore the Council of Trent became more of a survival or endurance issue for the Catholic Church. The disputes were hotly debated over a period of 22 years. Here are some of the issues on the agenda; <u>condemn the doctrines of Protestantism and clarify the teachings of the church on all disputed points.</u> The emperor had requested that Protestants were to be present but that did not happen. Another topic was to deal with <u>reforming the administration of the church, the papacy had become corrupt which had infiltrated the bishops & priests</u>. The church was to be the <u>ultimate interpreter of Scripture</u>, <u>Luther's doctrine of justification by faith alone</u> must be clarified by the council, as well as <u>indulgences</u>, <u>pilgrimages</u>, <u>veneration of saints</u>, <u>relics</u>, <u>veneration of the Virgin Mary</u>, all was affirmed, although indulgences were only to be given for good works. The council closed with a series of ritual acclamations honoring the reigning Pope, the Pope who had convoked the Council, the Emperor, and the kings who had supported it, the papal legates, the cardinals, the ambassadors present, and the bishops followed by acceptance of the faith of the Council and its decrees, many of them denouncing the heretics. The number of attending bishops opened with 30 but increased toward the close in 1563. The affirmed decrees were signed by <u>255</u> members.

FIRST VATICAN COUNCIL (523)

The early church councils up to the 1500's, before the Reformation, were often convened by the emperor who charged the delegates to clean up false teachings in the church that kept inching forward to demoralize the real Biblical faith that had been inculcated into the church believers since the days of the apostles, Timothy was facing such adversity in 2 Timothy 2: 17-18. Since then the Councils were mandated to deal with these issues. After the Reformation most agenda items were related to specific Catholic doctrines such as <u>confessions</u>, <u>popes</u>, and <u>contemporary church problems.</u> So why are we talking about it here? We have friends, co-workers, and neighbors, or interfaith marriage issues. Here is what happened at the First Vatican Council. It was convened by Pope Pius IX on 8 Dec, 1869 to deal with specific problems, such as <u>rationalism</u>, <u>liberalism</u>, and <u>materialism</u>, so far we can agree, as these controversies have surfaced in all churches; some more then others. When the council took up these issues, as well as secularism, naturalism, modernism, and pantheism, they condemned all of them with minimal comments. After the deck was cleared then came the hot and major controversy of the entire meeting; it was <u>the Popes authority</u>, *not* whenever he speaks, but *<u>only as he speak ex cathedra to the whole church in the power of Jesus Christ free from error; and when he speaks on faith, moral, and doctrinal issues</u>* only then *<u>the pope is infallible</u>*. That was a contentious issue and an agreement was far from unanimous. The majority of the council fathers, (urged on by

Pius IX) overrode perhaps the most vociferous opposition the counsel ever had to deal with. Although it was <u>approved</u>, there are still major disagreeable issues between the Roman church and Protestants, as well as a high number of the membership within the Catholic Church. The opposition argued that infallibility was never mentioned in the early medieval church, and pointed to various occasions in history when popes taught heretical doctrines; the most notable case was Honorius-I (625-638) who was condemned by the Third Council of Constantinople (680-681) and again by the 6th ecumenical council. Then there was the Papal Schism of 1378 when three popes could not agree who was the real pope and excommunicated each other. One of the major dogmas of infallibility is the Immaculate Conception of Mary the mother of Jesus; defined by pope Pius IX on December 8, 1854, it also has remained one of the most contentious issues among Catholic Church members as well as some clergy. That sums up most of the agenda of the First Vatican Council.

BELGIC CONFESSION OF FAITH (524)

The Belgic Confession was called that because it originated there. Its chief author was Guido de Bres, a preacher of the Reformed Churches. A copy was sent to king Philip II of Spain, along with a letter in which they declared obedience to the government and offer their backs to stripes, their tongues to knives, their mouths to gags, and their bodies to fire, rather than deny the truth expressed in this confession. They did not get their freedom. In the 16th century Christians were exposed to extreme, cruel, & severe persecution by the Roman Catholic Church who was controlled by evil, not by Christ. Today in the Western world religious tolerance exists where Protestants are for the most part dominant, and allow people the freedom to believe whatever they wish. Some said; that was not so during the years of the Crusades, but we disagree. From 1100-1300 a series of religious wars ignited among three groups, <u>Jews</u>, <u>Christians</u>, and <u>Muslims,</u> all claiming Jerusalem as *their* Holy City. While traveling through Jerusalem a few years ago it's clearly evident all three groups, *still* want control of the City which may be the reason tranquility has been elusive there. Christians are still persecuted throughout the world. North Korea is ruled by the little fat man who thinks he is god, in Pakistan Islam rules; in India Hinduism dominates; many such countries attempt to prevent Christians from practicing their faith, except where real

Christianity has control. Guido de Bres fell along with thousands who sealed their faith with their lives. The Belgic Confession was accepted mostly as is, by the Reformed Synod of Dort (1618–1619, (Dort means Dordrecht, a city in the Netherlands). The confession was adopted in to one of the doctrinal standard for the Reformed Churches. It consists of 37 articles most of which would be acceptable by serious Christians. The articles describe the belief in only one God, the Bible as the written Word of God, all 66 books, Old & New Testament as authority over all other books & canons and explains the difference between the inspired texts _vs_ that of apocryphal writings such as the books of Esdras, Maccabees, Tobit, and others. The sufficiencies of the Holy Scriptures offer the full counsel of the triune God the Father, Jesus, the Son, and the Holy Spirit, three persons, one eternal God who created and governs all things, Adam & Eve and original sin, fallen men, incarnation of Christ, sanctification by faith, elders, deacons, and ministers, and the marks of a true church vs. a false church (_which we will discuss separately_). The Belgic Confession of faith was initially written to secure freedom from persecution which was not attained. It was adopted by the National Synod of the Reformed Church held during the last three decades of the sixteenth century and embraced as doctrinal denominational statement along with the creeds and catechism.

TRUE CHURCH VS FALSE CHURCH (525)

This may be the topic we wished that was never selected and makes me think of the time when I sometimes stepped on the debate stage, when the topic was risky, (such as abortion at the university) and was told _Terry you walk where angels fear to tread_ referring to the 1905 novel by that title of Nobel Prize winning novelist Edward Morgan Forster; especially when you know the audience is: what psycho analysts call "being of two minds". Having said that we shall look at the marks of a true church, and here we go: There must be sound doctrine of the gospel of Christ which is preached; (we will not comment here about electronic technology), but believe that able members should attend worship services, as well as being known in the community for their Christian walk, whether employer or employee their practices reflect the love of Christ. Another is the administration of the sacraments, such as Baptism and The Lords Supper. With the latter every one needs to examine himself and whoever eats the bread and drinks the cup in an unworthy manner is eating & drinking judgment unto himself. The elder or pastor who administers the sacraments must make that clear; the Scripture does not require membership in that church but it does require a contrite heart. A Christian is not free from sin, but is asked to examine their heart and humble ourselves before God, confess our sins and be assured that sins are forgiven. Then there is the issue of Baptism and it is *there* where angels fear to tread; serious Christian leaders of major denominations have not agreed on the issue of infant baptism, many practice it; such as; Catholics, Eastern Orthodox churches, as well as Anglicans, Lutherans, and Presbyterians, Congregationalists, Reformed, Methodists, Nazarenes, Moravians and many more. Several of these churches let people decide whether or not they want to baptize their babies. Some call it christening, or wait till the child is of age. Then there is the issue of church discipline. This requires church leaders to follow the Biblical mandate of advising, warning, and apply discipline, such as prohibiting access to communion. When all else has failed the last resort is excommunication and there is a process in place for re-admission after church elders are satisfied that true repentance has taken place. In summary the true church consists of regenerated believers in Jesus; has qualified leaders; gathers for worship; preaches the Word, administers the Sacraments, committed to Jesus, serve people who are sinners saved by grace. The church is not a social club although fellowship is vital. It is a place where true believers congregate, support each other, worship God and confess Christ as Lord and Savior.

WESTMINSTER CONFESSION OF FAITH (526)

In 1643 the English Parliament called upon Learned, Godly, and Judicious Divines and asked them to meet at Westminster Abbey in order to provide advice on issues of worship, doctrine, government, and discipline of the Church of England. That brought together an assembly of 151 theologians, mostly Presbyterians and Puritans that met over a period of five years and produced a Reformed Confession of faith as well as a Larger and Shorter Catechism, which is now referred to as the _Westminster Confession of Faith_. That instrument is the standard doctrine for the Church of Scotland and has for more then four hundred years been adopted by myriad of national & international churches who have made it their own confession. It is meticulously formulated so that several denominations, such as Baptists, Congregationalists, and others have used adaptations of the Confession as a basis for their own doctrinal statements; although it is subordinate to the Bible the Old Testament & the New Testament. Parliament had intended it to be the major document for the Church of England, but it did not turn out that way; Leaders of the Church of England had pushed for adoption of the Act of Uniformity (1662 a move that Established the Church of England as the only legally approved church which resulted in the fact that those who subscribed to the Westminster Confession became known as nonconformist.

However, the Scottish Commissioners who were present at the Assembly at the Westminster Abby, they were satisfied with the Westminster confession of Faith and in 1646, that document had been sent to the English parliament to be ratified and submitted to the General Assembly of the Scottish Kirk. The Church of Scotland adopted the document, without amendment in 1647. In England the House of Commons returned the document to the Assembly requesting a list of proof texts from Scripture be included. It was forwarded to the Scottish Parliament who ratified it without change in 1690. The confession begins with a definition of the Bible as the written inspired Word of God, and is a systematic exposition of the Calvinist theology, influenced by Puritan and Covenant Theology and rules _out_ marriage with non-Christians. It further states that the Catholic mass is a form of idolatry, and civil magistrates have divine authority to punish heresy, and that the pope is the Antichrist, which was a common belief in 17th century England dating back to the 1500's when king Henry VIII, (after six failed marriages) had given the pope a piece of his mind & broke with Rome. Perhaps it's one of the reasons the pope was never seen at South Bay beach in England.

WESTMINSTER SHORTER CATECHISM (527)

The Westminster Shorter Catechism is a simplified version of Westminster Confession of Faith, which dates back to 1646. It was prepared in 1986, by several laymen associated with the First Presbyterian church in Mississippi. They enlisted theologians, who reviewed refined and assembled a committee of five, all of whom participated in the process of preparing this catechism, consisting of 107 questions & answers. Here are 13 of the 107: **1**. Q, what is man's primary purpose? _A_, Man's primary purpose is to glorify God and to enjoy Him forever. **3**. _Q_, What does the Bible primarily teach? _A_, The Bible primarily teaches what man must believe about God and what God requires of man. **10**. _Q_. How did God create man? _A_. God created man, male and female, in His own image and in knowledge, righteousness, and holiness, to rule over the other creatures. **14**. _Q_. What is sin? _A_. Sin is disobeying or not conforming to God's law in any way. **27**. _Q_. How was Christ humiliated? _A_. Christ was humiliated; by being born as a man and born into a poor family; by being made subject to the law and suffering the miseries of this life, the anger of God, and the curse of death on the cross; and by being buried and remaining under the power of death for a time. **33**. _Q_. What is justification? _A_. Justification is the act of God's free grace by which He pardons all our sins and accepts us as righteous in His sight. He does so only because He counts the righteousness of Christ as ours. Justification is received by faith alone. **39**. _Q._ What does God require of man? _A._ God requires man to obey His revealed will. **41**. _Q._ Where is the moral law summarized? _A._ The moral law is summarized in the Ten Commandments. **60**. _Q._ How do we keep the Sabbath holy? _A._ We keep the Sabbath holy by resting the whole day from worldly affairs or recreations, even ones that are lawful on other days. Except for necessary works or acts of mercy we should spend all our time publicly and privately worshipping God. **71**. _Q._ What does the seventh commandment require? _A._ The seventh commandment requires us and everyone else to keep sexually pure in heart, speech and action. **81**. _Q._ What does the tenth commandment forbid? _A._ The tenth commandment forbids any dissatisfaction with what belongs to us, envy or grief at the success of others, and all improper desire for anything that belongs to someone else. **83**. _Q._ Are all sins equally evil? _A._ In the eyes of God some sins in themselves are more evil than others, and some are more evil because of the harm that results from them. **86**. _Q._ What is faith in Jesus Christ? _A._ Faith in Jesus Christ is a saving grace, by which we receive and rest on Him alone for salvation, as He is offered to us in the gospel.

ONE VOTE (528)

Have you ever said: Why should I vote? What difference will one vote make? If that is you're thinking, it might be a good idea that you listen; especially _you_ who are generation X-ers, (_First generation to grow up with personal computers, are technologically adept, and very tech savvy_.) Please let me take you for a little tour and pay close attention to this in our history; can you imagine the feeling after an expensive & tiring campaign to loose by only none vote? Thomas Jefferson did not loose but was elected by one vote in the US House after the Electoral College was deadlocked, then on the final vote Jefferson was declared the winner over his opponent Aaron Burr. To add Texas to the Union (1845), California in 1850, Oregon in 1859, Idaho in 1890, all of these were approved by one vote in the US Senate. In 1867 one vote ratified the purchase of the territory of Alaska. Then there is the sad story of Cliff Farmer in Arkansas. He told his wife in the morning make sure u vote, she did, but _he_ himself got to the polls two minutes after it closed. He lost his bid for office by one vote, _his own_. In 1776 the recently formed nation in the new world had severed ties with the mother country and the question was: what language shall we adopt? We had been inundated by many new German immigrants and the vote was a tie; shall we adopt as our national language _German_ or _English_. The deadlock was finally broken when one German delegate changed his vote and voted with the British and the English language was adopted to be the official language only by one vote. In 1868 impeachment proceedings were brought against President Andrew Johnson for abuse of powers; the final vote declared him innocent, but only by one vote. Here is a major issue that was costly in 1649 for King Charles 1 of England. The vote in Parliament was 68 for and 67 against; the king lost his head by one vote, and was beheaded, even though the vote was by the narrow margin of one vote. France had been established as a monarchy, but there was a strong movement to get away from a king and 1875 the French parliament voted to get out of the monarchy and become a republic; but it required every vote in the chambers when the final vote came in it was a success but only by one vote. In 1923 members of an obscure new political party met in the Munich beer hall and elected ex-soldier Adolph Hitler who was a young and promising upcoming leader who had mastered the art of public speaking and was elected to new leader of the Nazi Party. The vote was not overwhelming he was elected by just one majority vote, although after that, elections were no longer important. Pres. Reagan said: "Freedom is never more then one generation away from extinction."

FOSTER CARE. ORPHANAGES OR ADOPTION (529)

Foster care, orphanages, or adoption, China seems to place children in orphanages while America and the Western world are more supportive of Foster Care and adoption. What is best for the child? Here is what we discovered after numerous China visits. When a child lives in an orphanage does not mean the child has no parents, many do! Some parents are not able to raise them, some even have abandoned the child, or left the baby at the doorstep of a children's home. According to their own stats, China has about 500,000 orphans in a nation of 1.5 billion people, however we can not verify that, some of these children suffer from various diseases, or other health issues and China provides no medical assistance for the poor, or the handicapped, many orphanages are highly lacking in the proper education and medical resource needs for disabled youngsters; some of the newborn _were_ wanted, some may be girls and 80% of the people want boys. Some children are living in senior homes, it is what we would call the grand parent concept; a ten year old must consent to the adoption, and even after that, if the relationship deteriorates it can be terminated; children over 14 have to find work. We have had personal contact with an abused child in Guangdong who can speak English and we have communicated with this eight year old on a weekly phone conversation with no need of an interpreter over a period of about 16 years since she was 8 and is now 24; she was an incest victim of both parents. China had a one child policy since 1980 and for various reasons the government was forced to end it in 2016; but that was not all, in 2021 the National Health & Family Planning Commission issued a system of fines for violators such as local government officials who had pressured women by the now Communist government who loves to exercise total control over its people. From one extreme to another China has adopted a three child policy. We also visited Korea and there seems to be more activity with International Adoption programs, but having traveled China several times we are more familiar with the programs there. We ourselves, (here in Hawaii), have cared for several foster children over a number of years, and believe for the sake of these children the best approach should always be to adopt, but some are not adoptable. Most children want to belong to a family which some never had. Those saw our Foster children knew that we were not their birth parents, and could feel the shock waves go through the child when: (may be unintentional), uncouth questions were asked, about us not being their real parents. The child would cringe at the insensitive comments about our racial, and age difference; children want to belong to a family of their own, it gives them security.

DEPT OF EDUCATION, DO WE NEED IT? (530)

At the time the Constitution was written, education was not even considered a function of local government, let alone the federal government. There is no reason to put education under the commerce clause. Local governments should do only those things that individuals cannot do for themselves, state governments should do only those that local governments cannot do; education is something that individuals acting alone and cooperatively _can_ do. To put it somewhat bluntly, I do not think the Department of Education is constitutionally legitimate, let alone appropriate. I would favor abolishing it and while we are at it, would throw out the Department of energy as well. But that is another story. I first got involved in the 1960's during Johnson's Great Society Programs and bringing with it a large scale involvement of the Federal Government, and the parents stepped back and let the government take over. It seems that there was some real education after the 1940's but that changed when the Federal government got more involved in the school. Perhaps President Ronald Reagan said it best during his August 12, 1986 news conference when he said: "*The nine most terrifying words in the English language are: "I'm from the government and I am here to help,*" These few words said more then I could say in 1 hour, it underscores the reality that President Reagan was one of the finest communicators we may have ever had in the

White House. He did not go the media but went directly to the American people with whatever was on his mind. I recently saw a speech by Betsy De Vos who served as Secretary of Education and paid attention when she supported reducing the department's authority, even went so far as to say: "I personally think the Department of Education should not exist" while she spoke at the first N*ational Moms for Liberty* summit over the weekend. *Moms for Liberty* is a conservative nonprofit founded in Florida to help advocates for parents to have more influence over public school decisions. The organization received much national attention when it fought against mask mandates in schools and again when they opposed curriculum related to LGBTQ rights, race, and discrimination. DeVos has repeatedly spoken against the Department of Education. We spent 3 days privately with her father in law in Los Angeles I understand her thinking and am in total agreement with her. When she was pressed to explain how the people felt that work in the department she said there are very few who get the work done that is needed; we have 4,400 employees working there at a budget of $68 billion a year and my 2 questions are: Do we need them? How much do these 4400 people know what my children should learn in Hawaii vs. a local school board of parents?

ASTROLOGY–THE $100 MILLION HOAX (531)

Here are some interesting facts: according to _USA Today of June 20, 2000._ About 41% of Americans believe in Astrology, and are spending according to _Business 2.0_ about $100 million a year on discovering their future. Do you want to know your future? When I was about 10 or 11 years old I asked the prettiest girl in school if she would marry me, and she said _NO._ So I asked mom if she would change her mind for me. Mom always had patience even though she spent many years on her sickbed with MS (an illness we knew nothing about); it took mom's life in her early 40's. She told me kindly; perhaps I should wait about 15 years. I told mom: she may change her mind and marry Pete who twice beat me in the running competition, I can't wait that long, in 15 years I will be 26 and may have long died of old age. Mom was more right then she may have realized, it took about that long for the right lady to come into my life. It is normal to be anxious about our future. Mom said: _ask God._ Astrology dates back to about 2000 years before Christ in Babylonia. In the Scriptures, in Isaiah 47 God warns us against going to Astrologists who can not even save themselves, but we prefer to be deceived. Think of this: Why Astrologers have never accepted the generous financial offers of Fame & Fortune and much free publicity. As far as I know the offer may still be open. I think it was _Time_ or _Life magazine_ that offered free publicity to any astrologer or just anyone who would predict 7 out of 10 national, or international events. Here are some, **1**: which continent will have the next major national disaster; **2**: Next famous male or female to commit suicide; **3**: from which state will the next Miss America come; **4**: what will be the next breakthrough in a major medical discovery; **5**: from which state will come the next man or woman of the year; **6**: what is the next major break break-trough in space technology, these are some that were offered. Perhaps you say; mariners have been guided by the stars for centuries; but that is astronomy and is very different from astrology. Professor Dr Charles Wahl of psychosomatic medicine at UCLA Neuropsychiatry institute said this: "I've seen astrology and the reliance on horoscopes do decided psychological harm; in that astrology is a system of belief maintained without any shred of scientific proof, it does incredible harm and gives charlatans enormous advantage in preying on the minds of the easily influenced." A 1999 internet report revealed that horoscope and astrology are the most searched topics on the internet. If you must find your future in the stars, then gaze upon the star of Bethlehem. It points to the Christ who tells you there is a warm & loving God waiting, and its more reliable then reading about your horoscope.

GAMBLING (532)

Gambling is taking risk and there is a right and wrong way to take risk? A Christian should never gamble; here is the first question; is it wrong to invest in the stock-market, or buy Mutual Funds? There is a key difference between gambling and investing, although you can _win_ or _loose_ much in both. If you buy shares in Hawaiian Air, you hope the market will go up, then you both gain. If you play poker with friend Sam, you hope he looses and you win, _that's the key difference_. Gambling violates the Biblical Principal of loving your neighbor. Our comments here do not come from books, but are based on personal visits to the casinos in, Monaco, Las Vegas & Macao while visiting or attend business meetings, even discovered casino owner Stanley Ho in Macao, (just like us), never gambled. He was our client and became a friend. Here are our thoughts: **1**: Gambling creates no new wealth, is non productive, and is a parasite, **2**: Gambling depresses legitimate business siphoning money from the regular business community, **3**: Gambling is a sophisticated form of stealing, **4**: Gambling increase welfare costs and weakens the stability of family life, **5**: Gambling produces human desperation, leads to bribes, extortion embezzlement, corruption of legitimate sports, **6**: Gambling produces the wrong attitude toward work and creates the idea one can live by luck without making any contribution to society, **7**: Gambling contradicts social responsibility, mature adults seek to minimize risks, Gambling destroys security & increase risks, **8**: Gambling revenues violate all sound standard theories of taxation, **9**: Gambling as a source of state revenue has a consistent record of colossal failures in New Hampshire, New York, and even in Nevada, **10**: Gambling is socially and politically corrupt, morally dangerous and creates corruption in politicians, and corrupts governments, Gambling increases crime, attracts underworld hoodlums. Here is our experience: In the early 1970's there was a bill introduced in the Hawaii State legislature to make gambling legal in Hawaii, we took the lead opposing that, and received a surprise-call from US Atty Robert Fukuda offering legal counsel. He had served in the Hawaii State House and was willing to contact the Nevada Attorney General asking him to come and testify and he said yes. One day later he called again and said: "My office received an anonymous call: "If you go and testify in Hawaii, do not expect to find your wife & children to be alive upon return, I know the source and its real and do not want to sacrifice my family and need to cancel." Leaving u to ponder this question: Is that what we want?

GLOBAL WARMING, CLIMATE CHANGE, OR FIRE & ICE (533)

The year was 1895 and in the preceding 100 years the print media predicted major crop failures and billions people will die; just as the weather has changed over time, so has reporting! Following the ice age threats from the 1800's, fears of an imminent ice catastrophe were compounded in the 1920's. The concern lasted well in to the decade and beyond. It did not happen, but the predictions were real; there was great fear that the earth could plunge into an ice age. It sold a lot of newspapers; and the government said it was _real_, therefore it was serious, all climatologists agreed, and snow cube ornaments illustrated that the ice age was obliterating an unfortunate city. People were pleading for wildlife that faced certain & imminent doom; the idea of a world wide deepfreeze snowballed. Science fiction authors embraced the opportunity with books like "_The coming ice age_" or "_The World in Winter_", "_Rich countries of the North broke down under the ice_." Magazines with headlines such as "_Machines have stopped as people went south_." Books became best sellers with titles like: _Teeth Shattering_, a _Rogue arctic iceberg becomes a world menace_. Some illustrators showed Canada being one large block of ice with New York high rises having frozen water-levels up to the top floors predicting mass starvation. The pressures were unbearable, and for some suicide was the only way out. Getting the government involved to control the weather is not a new concept. According to the

Times January 19, 1975 the program would start at $18 Million a year increasing to $67 million, ($200 million in today's dollar). Suggestions how to re-route large Siberian Rivers, will be costly but if we are to survive, it must be done. In the 1970's reputable researchers worried policy-makers so much that scientists at the National Academy of Sciences meeting proposed the evacuation of 6 million people and migrate them south. But now the pendulum has swung the other way and 27 European climatologists have become worried that the warming trend may be irreversible. The November 13, 2000 Time magazine had the answer; and here it is; "*Increase the Government and make if bigger*." They can start planning immediately and save us all; magazines can begin to prepare us from the inevitable threat of the upcoming global heat waves, ***now on a serious note***: Two reporters writing *Fire & Ice* researched this issue for the preceding 150 years and discovered that the earth warms & cools a few degrees about every 25 years and from the wisdom of those reporters we can surmise God put us on this earth and has no intention of going on a vacation while we *freeze* or *burn* here. We may not be climate scientists but common sense tells us that God created, and has been managing the earth, since He created it thousands of years ago and has promised us to end it some day and take us out of here.

MINIMUM WAGE (534)

In June 2022 the governor of Hawaii signed a bill to raise the minimum wage from $10 to $18. Conservatives are skeptical about that, and liberals love it. The difference is that a large number of the conservatives for the most part are the job creators, even though they themselves have been working for years from sunrise to sundown at no wage for 6 or 7 days a week just to get a small business established. When after many years there finally is a small amount of success, you get a knock on the door and a person telling us: we are from the government and (in the words of pres. Reagan): we are here to help. It is at that point, you need to run the other way. This wage mandate is pontification by the government what I should pay my staff, and raises some serious questions. Why do we need to be told how much I should pay by someone who never had to make a payroll? It has the flavor of socialism and is opposite from the American spirit; we left that behind and now live the American dream of owning a small business. I paid staff based on their value, the labor market is competitive, and every new hire was advised: if u are as good as u say, you will never leave us for money; subsequently one person stayed on for 45 years and another stayed 18 years and only lost some due to family transfers by military spouses, but never in 50 years lost one who needed more money. 29 states and the District of Columbia have increased their wage by government mandate per FSLA of $7.25. Perhaps I am a little naïve but still have some serious questions. If Mc Donald pays its workers $5, and Burger

King pays $5 and Starbuck pays $5 and the government pays $6 to take the unemployment line, where would the worker want to apply? That situation would be more like Communist China or North Korea, under Marxist rule but you have security from the cradle to the grave; your job would be secure and as long as you put in the time you'd have no worries but we live in America and here there is _risk_ along with unlimited opportunity _if you want it_. In America you need to earn your wages and are required to produce, and if successful there are great rewards. Having lived under both systems it saddens me to tell you that we are sliding back to the king, rater then embracing the democracy of which we are all recipients. This is America and Washington has a rotating president _not a king_. Rather then a minimum wage mandate I prefer a suggestion box in every business offering _all employees_: _how can we improve_? If your suggestion is _implemented_ you will be rewarded from $100 to $10,000, or a promotion, determined by value to the business, as a small business owner I would have paid it with pleasure.

ELECTORAL COLLEGE (535)

The Electoral College concept is now open for debate again, and at first glance why should I give up my right to vote for the President of the United States, and give that to an elector who I do not know who will cast my vote and that vote may not even be my choice? Living in Hawaii, I know it will not be the person I would choose as my President. However it is comforting to know that the person who travels to the capital can not be a legislator; we have often thought, why not cast our ballet by popular vote meaning <u>one vote per person</u>. The Founding Fathers did look at that too in 1776 when the population was about 3 million, (now it's about 330 million), and here is what they came up with. The states with the most people would always choose the president such as California, Texas, Florida, New York, & Illinois most of them quite liberal, would vote for a president and we in Hawaii might as well stay home. To solve this dilemma here is the amazing genius solution the founders came up with: They chose: _The Committee of Eleven_ and _they_ proposed the Electoral College. That is a system where each state gets a number of electoral votes based on the most recent Census. Here is what that looks like now: Hawaii, Idaho, New Hampshire, and Maine each get 4 electoral votes, Wyoming, Alaska, Utah, Arkansas, and Iowa each get 6, Illinois & Pennsylvania each get 20, South Dakota and Vermont get 3 each, New York and Florida get 29 each, and California gets 55, Michigan and Georgia get 16 each. The total Electoral votes for all the 50 states are 538, and to elect a president a majority is needed which are 270. The Electoral College division is not based on land size because that would go to Alaska & Texas. The number of electors is re-evaluated every ten years. In order to maintain a balance in the various branches of the Federal Government, members of Congress and government employees can not be electors and to further keep it separate the delegates are to meet in their home state preventing any federal intervention. After the election the electoral delegates must travel to Washington DC and cast their vote in the House Chambers on January 6 following the election. What if the electors cast their vote but do not have a majority. That becomes a problem, but they did think of that. The next step is; now the issue gets thrown in to the House of Representatives, (not the Senate), and based on the current perilous political situation in Washington we are tempted to think: May be the founders need to come back & rethink this part; they may not have been thinking of a speaker of the house with "*eternal life*", the current one has already been in that position over 15 years. The Electoral College is a complicated system but we believe this information is accurate.

IMMIGRATION REFORM (536)

According to Homeland Security America experienced 2 million illegal border crossings last year and these are those we know about, these are people who do not go through the normal process, like all of us had to do. What did we have to do to get in here during the 1940's & 50's? Here are *some* of our requirements: **1**: being waitlisted for 7 years, **2**: needed a US sponsor, <u>or</u> bring in enough cash to support ourselves for 5 years, proving that with a certified bank statement, **3**: A signed doctor certificate certifying we were in good health, **4**: Acknowledge that we could <u>not</u> apply for welfare or unemployment benefit the first five years, **5**: An FBI check proving that we had no criminal history and were squeaky clean **6**: a signed statement that we promised to contact immigration every time we moved, or at least report our address once a year. Wanting to be acceptable and do the right thing in the New World we faithfully did that. Upon entry we had $10,000 during the late 1950's (in today's money that is about $100,000). It eliminated the sponsor requirement, we were wiling to forego a salary and work on commission, meaning we worked sunrise to sundown 6 days a week. It was risky but turned out to be a blessing. During the 1950's it became clear that America was the great melting pot of diverse ethnicities and those of us who came out of Europe, had just left Hitler behind, and those who came out of the Asian countries had emerged from the Pacific war as well as seeing communism on the rise and saw an opportunity of liberty here wanting to be part of the great American experiment.

So why was America successful while much of the world remains in poverty? America was founded as a bold experiment never tried anywhere before and has demonstrated that a society governed by ordinary citizens that gives full expression to the ideals of liberty, justice and opportunity for all, can work. In for work we were given the opportunity to work and build a business that became our own and by comparison in Europe all we could see was many businesses go to heirs most of who would inherit it because he was the son, but in 9 out of 10 cases a worker would never get that option. A lot of that has changed since the 1950's. most of those who migrated to the New World became successful. The cost was hard work, & sacrifice, but the rewards far exceeded that what was offered in the home country. The immigrants of the 1940, 50's and 60's were the pioneers that made America the envy of the entire world. Now there are calls for immigration reform; we agree and suggest a re-visit of the immigration laws of the 1940'- 1960's and begin with securing the border, close all Sanctuary Cities, and deport all who are here illegally and have a criminal history.

TEN COMMANDMENTS (537)

The 10 commandments AKA the Decalogue are a set of Biblical laws relating to ethics & worship which play a fundamental role in Judaism, Christianity, and Islam; and include instructions to worship the only true God, to honor one's parents, to keep the Sabbath, as well as spell out prohibitions against idolatry, blasphemy, murder, adultery, dishonesty, theft & coveting. Religious groups follow different traditions for interpreting or numbering them. The Biblical narrative begins in Exodus 19, after the children of Israel coming out of Egypt arrive at Mount Sinai & were assembled at the base of the mountain, while their leader Moses ascended to the top; there was lightning & thunder and the mountain was covered with smoke because the Lord descended on it in fire; the mountain trembled violently, then the sound of the trumpet grew louder & louder and God spoke these words: I am the Lord your God, who brought you out of Egypt, out of the land of slavery; you shall have no other gods before me, you shall not make an idol in the form of anything in heaven above, or on the earth beneath, or in the waters below. You shall not bow down to them, or worship them, for I the Lord your God am, a jealous God, punishing the children for the sin of the fathers to the third & fourth generation of those who hate me, but show love to a 1000 generations of those who love me and keep my commandments. You shall not misuse the name of the Lord your God, for the Lord will not hold anyone guiltless who misuses the name of the Lord your God, for the Lord will not hold anyone guiltless who misuses his name; remember the Sabbath day by keeping it holy. Honor your father & mother. You shall not murder, do not commit adultery, you shall not steal, and not give false testimony, and you shall not covet anything that belongs to your neighbor. We have several questions about this. Why in America today is this so controversial? Why a monument or any sign that displays these must, be torn down? For decades a number of states have been entangled in legal disputes whether or not the Ten Commandments can be displayed on public or private property, although it is the fundamental legal code of Western Civilization and the common law of the United States. Before all the rules of metal detectors, we could freely walk through these buildings and were able to see these magnificent and artistic displays who have served our nation for centuries. These are the people's buildings and should be open and accessible to all. Misguided judges in some states have ruled that they are harmful and ordered them removed from Court buildings and public display, and prohibited in our schools. Are our leaders afraid that some people may try to obey them, and harm our children?

AMERICAN EXCEPTIONALISM (538)

American Exceptionalism is an <u>idea;</u> indicating that America is inherently different from other nations. Proponents of this argue that the values, of the political system, and the historical developments, are unique in human history, and point to the fact that America is a distinct nation founded upon an ideology not established anywhere else on the world stage. It was the foreign minister of France, Alexis de Tocqueville, (while analyzing the living standards and social conditions of individuals as well as their relationship to the market and state in Western societies), who was the first writer following his travels to describe the country as exceptional. Although critics on the left have argued that American history is morally flawed because of its slavery practice, civil rights, and social welfare issues, claiming they lack virtue especially in dealing with Native Americans, and people of color, all of which do not conceal US inconsistencies. However the founders had a very distinct idea of the moral order, and believed that morality and government should be in harmony with the "laws of nature, and natures God". Natural law is universal and thus morally binding on all mankind, and they said repeatedly that freedom can not be enjoyed without virtue. Without it, you get tyranny based on power and selfishness. Governments must protect the natural rights and liberties of their people; it is where the idea of limited government comes from. It's why they used checks & balances and the idea of equality before the law did not mean <u>equal income</u> but meant equal opportunity to pursue happiness. There is no American ethnicity, only a mixture of English, Dutch, Scandinavian, German, African, Asian, Jews, Arabs and other. There is total freedom of religion and to understand how unique America is, look at the cultural difference among immigrants not learning English, but buying land, and living the American dream, all diverse blended into unity; with unique rights of individuals not found anywhere in the world. We have, and still do, sacrificed the men & women of our armed forces to liberate other nations from aggressive invaders, and do not seek territorial gain, but aid in establishing liberty around the world, which originated during the American Revolution from which the US emerged as a new nation with a distinct ideology based on liberty, equality, individual responsibility, sound market based economics, all perceived both domestically and internationally as superior having the unique mission to help transform the world. That is American Exceptionalism, certainly not flawless, but also not paralleled anywhere else in the world.

RELIGIOUS FREEDOM (539)

Many of us are here because America is a free country that most likely was not so where most of us came from, and may be one of the reasons we are here. Let's see where we are now? Our U.S. Supreme Court seems to be the final arbitrator of the issues listed here, should we ask them to take a look at these? **1**. It is graduation time; young people are not permitted to give credit to Jesus, and the traditional graduation opening prayer, is MIA. **2**. Ten Commandments are outlawed in school, even monuments that display them are removed, (see Judge Roy Moore Alabama), there seems to be a great fear that some may want to obey these rules.**3**. _Manger-scenes_ historically displayed in shopping malls at Christmas time; no longer anywhere, not only have they been removed but are outlawed in virtually every American mall. **4**. Prayer is banned in public schools. **5**. Friday night football prayer is not allowed, coaches who pray are punished, even a coach who silently prayed in the field, could be seen in the distance, was fired, (although the court later reversed that ruling). **6**. Christian students banned from passing out flyers at flagpole. (Very similar to what Sophie Scholl did in Nazi Germany, passing out leaflets in her school for which she was executed, (_see 83 in book #1_) **7**. Traditional prayers removed from military academy **8**. Most (if not all) city council and legislative meetings were historically opened with prayer; not so now, it is outlawed in all 50 states. **9.** According to the _Washington Times April 15, 2015_, Christians in large numbers are leaving the military which has become a "_hostile_" work environment; that will not allow them to express their religious belief; military chaplains are punished for Biblical Counseling. **10**. _Jan. 2016_, Christian soldier posted a Bible verse and was _court-martialed_ for that. Military cemeteries across America are under pressure to remove crosses. Any public gathering, prayers have been tossed out; if done, can not conclude with "_in Jesus name_". The Pledge of Allegiance lines "_under God_" ruled unconstitutional, by some courts. If you take a walk through the nation's capital, you can't miss the fact that our founders were religious people, it's everywhere; in order to make it an anti Christian environment it would need have to be scrubbed clean to please a few self proclaimed atheists. My question is: I have stood at the border of North Korea, and the whole world could see when Otto (_22 yr old American student_), was returned by the NK soldiers claiming he fell in a coma after being sentenced to 15 years hard labor, for what? _Taking a poster_, he died for that crime. North Korea cleansed most of their nation of any semblance of Christianity; we left ideologies such as that, abandoned that world, and came here to taste and experience _real_ freedom.

STATESMEN VS. POLITICIAN (540)

The difference between a statesman & a politician is like eating vegetables & ice cream; vegetables, may not taste good all the time, but they're mostly good for you, politicians are like ice-cream, everybody loves them, but you don't know why u got sick. Our country was founded by Statesman such as John Adams, & James Madison; both had virtually no political experience when they were elected to the Continental Congress but they had _Ideas_, _Education, Conviction,_ and _Character_. Madison's silent labor and Adams' brilliant oratory skills did what all the experience in the world could not do; they gave us _Liberty_ and the most brilliantly devised system of _Self-Government_ in history. The founders were principled men convicted of an ideology, and were held in high esteem. No threat of death or pain could deter them from their dream of building a Constitutional Republic that would guarantee Liberty & Justice for all. In simple terms a politician works with details and a statesman works with ideas. A politician wants to make sure this will get him re-elected; a Statesman wants to know if it's good for the health of the country. A politician wants to raise the minimum wage; a statesman says the government has no such control; the market place will determine that. A politician wants to know how much will it cost and asks, will this get me re-elected, he follows the crowd, lives & dies with his finger in the wind, and floats ideas based on what will assure keeping him in office, A statesman does not survey, but knows what is needed then leads and stands by his conviction, he builds his platform on a foundation of firm unchanging fundamental truths, things he believes at his very core, he is like a building with a fixed foundation that stands on bedrock principles. A politician puts out his antenna, than makes his decisions based on which way the wind is blowing. A statesman follows his moral compass which is rooted in absolute moral rights & wrongs. A statesman _earns_ his support; a politician campaigns for it; a statesmen loves the Constitution and is convicted that power should be in the hands of the people; a politician likes having power over the people. A statesman serves 1 or 2 terms, then steps back, and practices term limits, and let others serve. A politician when elected enjoys the prestige and does not want to give it up and is opposed to term limits, he engages in party politics and generally leaves office in better financial condition then when he came in, a statesmen leaves office financially in the same condition he came in. We are flooded with politicians and experience a famine of statesmen, where have they gone?

THE BIBLE (541)

The bible was written while the greater part of the world was still uncivilized so how could it speak to us today? Think of this; It was penned on 2 continents, written in 3 languages its composition & compilation took 16 centuries and its 1 book, 1 system of doctrine, 1 code of ethics, 1 plan of salvation, & 1 rule of faith; parts were written in tents, deserts, cities, prisons, palaces, & dungeons, at different times & under varying circumstances, in times of imminent danger & seasons of great joy. Among its writers were judges, kings, priests, prophets. Patriarchs, prime ministers, shepherds, scribes, soldiers, teachers, physicians and fishermen, some were scholars others just simple folks. God used 40 sinful imperfect people and produced one infallible book, in which with great authority is presented the plan of Redemption as central, fundamental & in unity. The Bible has been read by more people in about 7000 languages, more than any other book. Genesis presents creation, the fall of men and the need for a Redeemer; followed by a system of elaborate sacrifices and offerings representing the nature of Redemption; then we stroll by the prophets, even Jonah, (the only prophet who did not like his job), and Isaiah who wrote that 53rd chapter as if he was sitting at the foot of the cross. Jeremiah stood before kings & forecasted coming disasters & Ezekiel lived in exile during international upheaval when Assyria destroyed the Northern Kingdom; Hosea was told by God to marry a prostitute to symbolize Gods willingness to heal the relationship with his people who had committed adultery when she ran away, God told him to go to the slave auction and buy her back; then we meet Amos who earned his living from the flock as well as being a tree trimmer; Micah forecasted about a little town named Bethlehem from where the Messiah would come & summarized Gods requirements to do justice and walk humbly with God. Habakkuk was a unique prophet who questioned God how he could do the things he did and still be God. Malachi rebukes the people for doubting God & exhorts them to be faithful in giving and serving. Then God is silent for 400 years, after that we walk in to the New Testament where the Gospel is explained in 4 different ways setting forth the basis of Redemption namely the incarnation, life, death, resurrection & ascension of the Redeemer followed by the book of Acts illustrating the redemption power. Then follows a series of letters explaining that salvation is for Jew & gentile & finally the book of Revelation showing us the ultimate triumph. God used 40 imperfect humans producing 66 books condensed into one book of men's need for a Redeemer and God's provision of that Redeemer.

BRITISH COMMONWEALTH, NEW ERA (542)

The Queen is dead; her son Charles is the new king, England and the Commonwealth move into a new era, at very tenuous times. During the 70+ year reign of Queen Elizabeth much has changed in the 54 commonwealth countries. We have lived in, and visited many of these nations, in Africa, Canada, the Caribbean, as well as the South Pacific nations of Australia, New Zealand, Fiji, and we believe the new king will have a Hercules task to keep some of these countries within the British Commonwealth, especially those that were colonies of Great Britain where much racial tension has surfaced. We agree with veteran journalist Christiane Amanpour who was born in England but mostly raised in Tehran till age 11 and has covered for CNN most Middle Eastern hot spots, and there have been many. She raised some serious questions about King Charles being able to relate to such groups as Black Lives Matter where much of the concerns date back to the colonial days which is undeniable history in some areas of the British Commonwealth. Even though Prince Charles has made some visits on behalf of his mother, he has essentially lived in the ivory tower of British Royalty and there are some serious questions whether or not he can relate to people who live in the real world. Britain has specifically had a controversial imperial history; people were in service to this empire and the wealth of the kingdom was primarily derived on the backs of their subjects;

Briton's are a multicultural nation and its citizenry will need to deal with all of such issues. That is <u>one</u> dilemma the new king will face. Then there is the pesky problem how he treated Diane who became one of the most popular members of the British Royals and gifted him with two handsome young boys. Will people forgive his infidelity? You might say it was a private matter, and failed marriages are common, but if you are on the public payroll it's not private. That brings us to issue nr three. In 1536 the pope denied a divorce to King Henry VIII resulting in the fact that he broke with the Holy See, seized all Catholic assets, and declared himself the <u>Supreme Head of Church,</u> renaming it *<u>The Church of England</u>* (or in most Commonwealth nations and the US, it's referred to as the *<u>Anglican Church</u>*. Although the king's daughter Mary, attempted to restore the English Church's allegiance to Rome, her attempt failed, and it remained the Church of England. Now that Prince Charles has been crowned <u>King Charles III,</u> he will inherit the title of <u>Supreme Governor of the Church of England.</u> Impressive, but is the new king ready for that? These are just three issues of which the results may be worth watching for; is the new king wise enough to rule the commonwealth?

GENDER REASSIGNMENT (543)

We could never have, even in our wildest imagination, anticipated that gender reassignment surgery would become a topic for discussion in our lifetime. Sweden became the first country in 1972 to allow it; they have a reputation of being among the worlds most tolerant nation about such issues, and published a study 29 years later in 2011 showing suicide rates are 19 times higher than average among those who had the procedure done. Gender Reassignment or Sex Reassignment Surgery refers to procedures to change your body from male to female _or_ visa versa by means of surgery; although the physical body may change, but hormonal balance that we received from our Creator will not be that simple. The California Teachers Association has adopted a position to allow a child to do that without parental consent and has received support of the Teachers Union although it is still not permissible to give aspirin to a minor child. What has become obvious that a large number of these teachers have no children of their own, but _do_ have an agenda for other people's children other then math, read & write. As a historical rule parental permission is required, for any medical procedure to a minor. Some time ago in Hilo there was a real live issue where a child got pregnant and the teacher took the child to an abortion clinic; the abortion was botched requiring immediate medical intervention. No doctor would touch the child without a parent present. The parents who were not aware (thinking their 12 year old daughter was in school), and they were visiting family in Kona. The girl was rushed to the Hilo hospital and needed immediate help to save her life but no doctor would touch her without consent of the parents who took the 3 hour drive back to be with their child. She had trusted her teacher to get a safe abortion, who had advised her not to tell your parents. The issue was to surgically remove an unborn child. With gender reassignment surgery we are talking about serious bodily harm with lifelong irreversible damage that can never be undone, all at the young age when a simple aspirin requires parental approval. Real parents give them authority to teach math, reading and writing. All medical procedures have always required parental consent but under no condition would a loving parent sign their child over to a teacher many of whom do not have children of their own but have their own agenda about other people's children. With gender reassignment remember this: God assigns the hormones to a male or a female and no surgery can change that, meaning a victim will have lifelong issues. The transgender movement is the latest phase of a Cultural Revolution grounded in secular worldviews repudiating the God of the Bible.

ENTEBBE: OPERATION RESCUE (544)

At one of our International meetings of Global Hope (GHNI) in Switzerland, I Terry Bosgra met Benson who was president of the Uganda Parliament; he asked me if I had ever heard of Entebbe? I said yes it is a small airport at Lake Victoria. For the next 3 days we chatted at every breakfast, lunch & dinner and became super friends he gave me his private phone and said: if you ever need anything in Uganda call me. "Terry had no idea he needed him so soon. After return to Hawaii received a call asking: Terry do you know anyone in Uganda, we are missionary dentists and are at the Uganda border and customs want so much bribe money we don't have it, can u help? I asked for a phone contact and said I will try, then called Benson and asked for advice. He said leave it to me, 3 hours later got a call: "*Thanks we are in, and no duties*". Now back to Entebbe. In June 1976 Air France Airbus Fl. A-300 with 248 Jewish & Israeli passengers from Tel-Aviv to Paris, was hijacked by the Palestine Liberation Army and diverted to Entebbe in Uganda. The flight stopped in Libya, where 58, (+4 hijackers), were let go, and then flew to Entebbe with support of Uganda's corrupt leader Idi Amin. All were left in the transit hall, an empty building. Israel was willing to meet their ransom demand, and asked for 3 days delay, giving them time to prepare 100 Commandos for a dangerous rescue mission. At that time the whole world learned it is never wise to tangle with the well trained Israeli Commando troops, who had first planned to drop the commandos with rubber rafts in Lake Victoria, but due to the many crocodiles there, they flew 4000-km (2500 miles), risking a well planned landing under the cover of darkness. As soon as they hit the ground, killed the guards and stormed the transit hall where the hostages were held, than yelled in Hebrew, (only understood by Israeli's), "*Every one on the ground*", The guards did not understand Hebrew, kept standing and were killed. 5 commandos were wounded their leader Jonathan, (brother of Benjamin Netanyahu), was killed. His body was loaded on the plane with all hostages. Some soldiers tried to intervene but were killed. When all were accounted for, the plane took off immediately under the cover of darkness back for the 4000 km return flight. The entire operation on the ground took 53 minutes. 5 commandos were wounded. Israel has not accepted Jesus, it's a small country entirely surrounded by enemy nations. It seems evident that God's protective arm was with the Entebbe operation, which may have been the most risky long range rescue plan ever attempted anywhere, with no friendly nations to land nearby. The nearest semblance may have been the raid on Tokyo led by Captain Doolittle on April 18, 1942 with converted B-25 bombers, but they could not return from the 650 mile flight.

CIVIL WAR (545)

In antiquity almost every country has experienced some type of civil war, but here we shall limit the rhetoric to the _American Civil war of 1861 to 1865_ which was the bloodiest and most divisive conflict while family fought family, brother against brother, resulting in the deaths of more then 600,000 people with millions more injured, leaving the south ruined and in shambles, not a happy ending. Although there were several issues, the central cause of that war was slavery, and whether or not that should be permitted to expand into western territories. Preceding to that war, was decades of political controversy which came to a head when Abraham Lincoln was elected to the office of President of the United States, and opposed expansion into the western territories; by 1840 more than 15,000 people were members of abolitionist societies in the United States and the topic became a popular expression of moralism which was the leading issue that led eventually to the Civil War. Pro and Anti slavery forces collided over the territories west of the Mississippi River. Abolition sentiment was not confined to religious or moral in origin; in 1863 when Lincoln issued the Emancipation Proclamation which declared all slaves to be free, applied to 3.5 million of the 4 million who were enslaved people at that time in the country, Lincoln explained his belief about this and said: "_If slavery is not wrong, than nothing is wrong._" Seven southern pro slave states seceded from the United States and formed the Confederacy and abolition continued to gain a strong foothold, but Lincoln's moderate approach succeeded in persuading 26 May, 1865 Border States to remain in the union; Southern Baptist & Northern Baptist split over the issue of slavery, and so were other Christian groups. Churches, Conventions, Newspapers and Reformers promoted an absolute and immediate rejection of slavery. Northern states were rapidly modernizing, invested heavily in diversifying, while the Southern states economy was based principally on plantations that produced a major share of the cotton and tobacco. Its labor force had been largely free. & the issue was not so much whether or not slaves should be free but could the country afford to lose a workforce that was almost free. At that time the abolition movement was like the ice in a glacier it was irreversibly pushing forward and became unstoppable. The nations most enduring anthems were born during the Civil War, when Virginia Howe heard the soldiers singing about John Brown's body she was disgusted and that same day began writing <u>The Battle Hymn of the Republic</u> which became the new version of the song that has lasted more then a century and is still popular today "*<u>Let us die to make men free.</u>*" When Lincoln signed the Emancipation proclamation, and the populace agreed, the Civil War was over and ended 26 May 1865.

KELLY FAMILY (546)

The Kelly Family is an Irish-American music group consisting of a multi generational family, usually 9 siblings who performed on stage with their parents. Their play was pop, rock, and folk music and toured Europe America from 1970's to about 2008. They sang in English, Spanish, and German. In 1990 they were ranked the 6th most popular music group having sold more then 20 million albums. They presented a ragamuffin and vagabonding lifestyle traveling around Europe in a double-decker bus and a houseboat. Their image was enhanced by their often homemade clothing enhanced by their very long hair worn by both male & female members of the band. The patriarch of the family Daniel Kelly Sr. has been described as a "*grizzled, ageing druid aesthetic*" but according to his daughter Kathy he was in earlier days "<u>a clean-cut intense conservative Catholic</u>" who studied for the priesthood. He married Joanne in 1957 and the couple left their native America in 1965 with their children and settled in Spain where Daniel opened an antiques shop. They separated and Joanne with son Daniel Jr., returned to America; in 1970 Daniel Sr. married Barbara Ann Suokko (<u>*Austrian Finnish heritage*</u>) from Massachusetts, and together they had 8 children. In 1974 they formed a band called <u>*the Kelly Kids*</u>; they learned different musical instruments and became popular in Spain, the Netherlands, Italy, and West Germany. All their money was stolen on one of the tours leaving them penniless. The family moved to Ireland living at a campground they toured again in a double-decker bus and later in a houseboat. Barbara was often performing with a newborn in her arms; they secured a contract to perform in Germany. Their major hit-song was David's song "Who'll come with me," singing the solo at age 12 with a Gaelic sounding melody at a time while Barbara was dying with breast cancer. The song was #1 on the chart in the Netherlands, Belgium & West Germany. They performed for the largest audiences Europe had ever seen. In 1995 one Vienna concert was attended by an audience of 250,000, that same year they filled Westfalenhalle in Dartmund which can seat 15,400 nine times in a row. In 2002 Papa Kelly died from a stroke and the Kelly family group began to dissolve and slowly the money began to disappear. The children got older and more independent. Some criticized their father for not giving them an education. Germany came after them about tax issues and the Dan Kelly Foundation was discovered not to be a registered charity, the family was mostly concerned with entertaining and none had considered the fact that all these countries have tax structures and rules. The parents are gone and none of the children are rich, the world enjoyed their music, even the houseboat and the double-decker bus are now gone, they blest the people but forgot the bureaucrats.

SEPARATION OF CHURCH AND STATE (547)

Many of us have our roots in Europe and for centuries monarchs have ruled by the idea of divine right. At the beginning of the Protestant Reformation, Martin Luther articulated a doctrine of two kingdoms the initial idea of separation of church and state. _Michael Sattler,_ one of the early Anabaptist leaders agreed with the hypothesis of two kingdoms, but wanted to take it in a whole new direction. In the early days of the Reformation movement, Anabaptists taught that believers should not vote, nor hold public office, or participate with the "kingdoms of this world." In 1534 king Henry VIII took it in a different direction. He was angry with the pope who refused to grant him a divorce; and broke with the Church of Rome, making himself ruler of the Church of England. Great Britain has retained ecclesiastical authority in the Anglican Church; King Charles is now Supreme Governor of the Church of England. I do not think that is what Martin Luther had in mind. Perhaps Thomas Jefferson, third president of the great American experiment was closer to what Luther was thinking. In many countries the two institutions of church and state remain, (and always have been), seriously connected. In the days of Jan Hus in 1415 it was clear the ecclesiastical cardinals and bishops of the church were elevated above the king, governors and kings were at the mercy of Bishops and Cardinals. Thank God for the 55 delegates to the 1776 Constitutional Convention in _The New_

World for sharp legal minds such as Thomas Jefferson the third US President who was able to navigate some clear paths through untested waters and lead the 55 delegates through areas where none had gone before. Following that, came the Bill of Rights adopted in 1791 as ten amendments to the Constitution of the United States, which may have been one of the earliest political expressions of religious freedom. Where could they go for clarity? England? But they wanted to get away from the king, and the Parliament, and begin a new experiment. The leaders of the new world had faith in Thomas Jefferson and his navigational ability in unchatered legal waters. It was the elders of the Danbury Baptist Association who asked for advice on Church/State issues and it was the response letter from Jefferson where he referred to "_building a wall of separation between Church and State_." We in America believe that religion is a serious matter between Man and his God. The metaphor of the _Wall of Separation_ became a part of the First Amendment jurisprudence of the US Supreme Court and was first used by Chief Justice Morrison Waite in _Reynolds v. United States 1878_. When America was born in 1776 there were 55 delegates navigating in unknown territory, America was an experiment that had never been tried anywhere before, because of these 55 men we are still here.

MOMS FOR LIBERTY *(MFL)* (548)

Moms for Liberty is an American conservative organization that advocates against school curriculums that mention LGBT rights, Critical Race Theory and other issues such as Gender re-assignment and others. It is a recent new grassroots organization. The group was founded January 2021 in Florida by Tina Descovich, Tiffany Justice, and some other school-board members. Their website was registered in 2020 and at their first national gathering in Tampa Florida in July 2022, _Moms for Liberty_ claimed to have 195 chapters in 37 states with a membership of about 100,000 members. Some governors like Kristi Noem, are members. The organization has been described as conservative, all the founders are registered Republicans, although the leaders claim that Moms for Liberty is nonpartisan however the organization is grounded in conservative values. They have praised Florida governor Ron DeSantis (along with other prominent Florida Republicans) who was their first speaker at the July 2022 gathering. One of their issues was a campaign against COVID-19 related health safety restrictions in schools, challenging mask mandates, and associated local policies. They broadened their agenda to encompass other school related items such as racism and religion that are addressed in the students reading material, some have called it _The Revolt of Mothers._ Left leaning Media Matters for America has accused MfL of using "Parental Rights" as a cover for harassing public schools, although accusations are flying in both directions, some claiming false child abuse cases, some carried signs saying: _Schools_ *are for Education*, *not for indoctrination*. We must continue to ask the question: *Who has the greater interest*, Teachers Unions? Or Parents? At one time I spent many hours on the debate stage and asked some leftist women this question: "How many children do u have? The overwhelming answers were often the same: "*I have no children*". As a father & grandfather I was always amazed that people who have no children feel a great need to dictate to me what is best for my children. (Having said that, the professor I have debated more then any other has two children). Critics have accused MfL making it more challenging for teachers to educate students. In 2021, the chair of one county told the DOE in a letter that the material on Critical Race Theory was in direct violation of the State Statutes. In one instance a mom who questioned the perverse sexual indoctrination in her daughters school was accused of being a terrorist at the School Board Meeting, and had to content with a visit by two FBI agents the following week. "When parents think their children are being educated, in some cases they may be indoctrinated and discipled by the "*powers of darkness*." Do we need *Moms for Liberty?* I think so.

TREATY OF WAITANGI (549)

The treaty of Waitangi is a document of importance to New Zealand history and its constitution. It was first signed on 6 February, 1840 between _the New Zealand Company_ acting on behalf of its settlers, and would be settlers, by William Hobson as consul for the British Crown and by Maori Chiefs from the North Island of New Zealand. It was drafted with the intention of establishing a colony in New Zealand when Maori leaders had petitioned the British for protection against French ambitions, as well as recognizing Maori ownership of their lands, forests, and other possessions, _and_ giving Maori rights of British subjects, and not feels that their rights had been ignored. Around 540 Maori, (including 13 of them women), signed the Maori language version, despite some of their own Maori leaders cautioning them not to sign it. Only 39 signed the English version. The preamble is written bilingual, although there were contentious issues due to the fact that some English words can not be translated in Maori, thereby creating strong disagreement resulting in _Maori/ New Zealand Wars_. Often the issues were about land deals, settlers were accused of occupying land that had not been sold. In the years following the treaty, the New Zealand government mostly ignored its content resulting in the fact that some required adjudication by the courts. We came in early 1960's and noticed a high number of such disputes were about real estate, (_This is my land_? or. _This is your land_? (Very similar what we later encountered in Hawaii). In 1975 the New Zealand Parliament passed the

Treaty of Waitangi Act, establishing the Waitangi Tribunal as a permanent commission of enquiry tasked with interpreting the treaty, researching breaches by the Crown or its agents and suggesting means of redress. Many recommendations of the tribunal are not binding on the Crown, but settlements as high as $1 billion have been awarded to various Maori tribes. As a result the treaty has become widely regarded as the founding document of New Zealand. (_Somewhat similar to America who established its Constitution as a founding document_). In 1974 the New Zealand government established _6 February_ as _Waitangi Day_ a national holiday to commemorate the date the treaty was signed. The first recorded contact between the Maori and Europeans occurred in 1642 when Dutch Explorer Abel Tasman arrived and was fought off. In 1769 English navigator Captain James Cook claimed New Zealand for the British Crown in a ceremony at the _Mercury Islands_ (small island, 8 km '_5 miles_' of the Waitangi coast of the NZ North Island, owned as a Private Island by two prominent NZ businessmen). The official NZ language is English, (_had Abel Tasman succeeded, it might have been Dutch_).

MAORI WARS (550)

In the 1960's we lived in Parnell, Auckland New Zealand (across the Street), from the War-Memorial-Museum, which became my favorite "_hang out;_" I learned about the history of the early British settlers and their subsequent battles with the Maoris who had come to NZ (_Aotearoa_) around the 1300's, meaning they had been there 5 centuries before the British (_Pakiha_) came. The cultures were very different resulting in conflicts which span a considerable period of time. The causes and outcome differed widely, especially in the early disputes of the 1840's while Maoris had been the predominant power for centuries before. During the 1300's they had come in several waves by canoe voyages from East Polynesia. After living several centuries in isolation, the Maoris had their own distinctive culture, whose language, crafts and performing arts evolved independently. (_some of them settled in the Chatham Islands, an archipelago about 430 mile east of New Zealand at one time slated to be under German control but is now administered by New Zealand_). We did not have computers in the 1950's and 1960's therefore on my free days I spent entire days in the War Memorial Museum, which was one of the first museums in NZ and in the South Pacific. In there I discovered a handwritten letter from a Maori Chief addressed to a British Captain, (due to our many travels have since lost that letter but here is the essence of it: "_Dear Captain we are doing well and invite you to have war with us. The hike to our settlement is a long journey, and your soldiers will be too tired to fight, therefore_ *we are inviting you to come a day early. you can rest and sleep. The next morning we have our battle; after that you can rest, stay the night, and hike back, Signed: Maori Chief.* This may not be 100% correct but it is the closest to what I can remember. Early contact between Europeans and Maori ranged from beneficial trade; the Maori began to adopt some of the new customs and technologies of these newcomers; the two cultures co-existed for about a generation. But then disputed land issues surfaced, escalating into serious conflicts such as <u>Wairau Affray</u>, <u>Northern War</u>, <u>Waikato-Invasion</u>, <u>Battle of Napier</u>, and many more till a solution was agreed to in the form of a treaty as discussed in other chapters here. The treaty was a short reprieve but there is still the pesky issue of assimilation into Western culture which was fiercely resisted and that will likely be an ongoing issue. Since we left, N Z has taken a dramatic shift toward trading with Asia. NZ population is now 65% *Pakeha* (European), 18% Asian, and 17% Maori. Have Maori wars ended? We are not too sure.

HOT WAR (551)

Most of us know about the *cold* war, but who can define the *hot* war? It is the war on energy which has two schools of thought, that are as far apart as the East is from the West, and is clearly reflected in the two major American Political Parties. D is Democrats moving towards Socialism where the philosophy is "*Government knows best*" and will always provide for us with Unemployment, Social Security, Health Care, Welfare, Sick Leave, Paid vacation, Maternity leave for men & women alike, even security if you don't want to work. It is a charitable way of taking care of each other. Although some of us are immigrants and have escaped from that ideology, came to the land of the free and the land of opportunity. The left embraces security, why not? Karl Marx built an entire society on such ideals, as expressed in Communist Manifesto, which are not all bad, but the new progressive generation has not experienced that, and believes America needs to make a giant leap to embrace these ideas. It means go back to foreign energy dependence and wean the US of fossil fuels; close the Keystone Pipeline, oil up all the windmills (*yes they need oil to run*), have solar panels on every roof, replace automobiles with electric vehicles and for the most part make use of public transportation then we can usher in Utopia, there will be no need for private ingenuity, *just let government do it*; the R party needs to get on board with such issues as the Green New Deal that was introduced in 2019, but has failed to advance. The president said we can do it with $40 Billion but AOC, (who has been in Congress one week) said: we need $93 Trillion and we can tax the rich more. To the R party, the most important issue in the environment is human health and comfort. The D party wants our gasoline powered vehicles eliminated and is working feverously to accelerate the process by increasing the tax on fuel, making it more difficult for the average American to operate an automobile. The war on energy is a real war and if the far left D Party succeeds, many of us will need to revert back to a bicycle. The president has declared war on American energy in a time of crisis; it's clear there is no unity for this destructive ideology with disastrous results clearly visible in North Korea where all ingenuity is stifled to serve the climate change dogma where _government knows best_. This is a hot war within our borders where the D party may succeed with only one possible success which is open borders, open voting booths for all residents, and accept the counsel of Joseph Stalin, who said: "Those who vote decide nothing; those who _count_ the votes decide _everything_." There u have it, two ideologies differing as far as day is from night.

COLD WAR (552)

We are in the middle of the Cold War, but who can define what it is? Some of us remember when Russia invaded Ukraine on 24 February 2022, or know a little about World War-II, 1940–1945, which raged on two fronts, Europe, and in the Pacific. In Europe it ended with the sketchy report of 30 April 1945 that Hitler had been killed with a self inflicted gunshot wound in the *Fuhrerbunker* in Berlin along with Eva Braun, (his wife of one day) who died with him by taking cyanide; their bodies were carried out of the bunker and burned. Exact details are not clear nevertheless, it effectively ended the war in Europe. In an attempt to end the Pacific War without a costly invasion of Japan, the US dropped two atomic bombs on the Japanese cities of Hiroshima and Nagasaki in August 1945. These two atomic bombings, together with the Soviet Union's declaration of war on Japan, convinced Emperor Hirahito to surrender to the Allies, which he did, and effectively ended the War in the Pacific. The use of atomic weapons at that time demonstrated America's technological superiority, who immediately assisted Japan to become a normal functioning nation again. That was followed by the Korean and the Vietnam wars, which cost many lives; although for the most part were local issues, even though some of us who have experienced loss of family members may disagree about the fact that both have largely remained regional. But the tensions with the Soviet Union, set the stage for a Cold War, which got us in a state of conflict between nations that does not involve direct military action but is pursued primarily through economic and political means, such as propaganda, acts of espionage, or proxy wars waged by surrogates. The term _Cold War_, as used today, is most commonly understood about tensions between America and the Soviet Union, (_now Russia_); although America and the Soviet Union were allies during WW-II, there were many tensions early on and once the common threat of Germany and Japan were removed it was only a matter of time before the shaky relationship deteriorated and we were faced with a possible new war, coined _"The cold war"_, with all attention on the race for the most effective nuclear arsenal. While testing such weapons as the Russian Tsar Bomba, which according to Russian leader Andrei Sakharov was 3,300 x more powerful then the atomic bombs used in Hiroshima and Nagasaki so powerful that it even scared the nuclear scientists in Russia who had designed such weapons; meaning if the "_Cold War_" is to continue it becomes vital who controls the nuclear code; the _White House_? or the _Kremlin_?

REFORMATION WALL (553)

On the grounds of the University of Geneva in Switzerland stands a giant monument called *The Reformation Wall*, which honors and depicts the giants of the Protestant Reformation who changed the history of the world forever. Being a student of the Reformation it made a deep impression on me and while I was chairman of the Global Hope Network International, which was headquartered in Geneva I could not resist going back there four more times. Many of these towering giants have left their footprints on the Reformation and are standing there as a monument for us to remember these historical witnesses to what took place several centuries ago in Christendom. The monument is built into the old city walls, and stretches for 100 meters and was inaugurated first in 1909 to commemorate the 400th anniversary of John Calvin's birth. Its location is designed to represent the integral importance of the fortifications and therefore of the city of Geneva. It was a culmination of a contest launched to transform that part of the park. Even though there are four primary figures who tower above the others, which are the four major figures of the Reformation standing five meter (16.4 ft) and are Calvin's main proponents, we might say they saw eye to eye theologically speaking, and are: William Farel (1489–1565), John Calvin (1509–1564), Theodore Beza (1519–1605) and John Knox (1513–1572), This being the hometown of John Calvin the theologians that are closest connected to his teachings are depicted here on the home territory of Calvin, standing shoulder to shoulder with him. Here Calvin is a giant spiritually but physically he suffered from ill health and died young just short of his 55 birthday, and was buried the next day in a grave that has been lost, his friend and also Calvin's pastor Theodore Beza preached the funeral sermon when Calvin died. Next to the three largest figures are the 3 meter figures: Frederick William of Brandenburg (1620–1688), William de Silent (1533–1584), Gaspard de Coligny (1518–1572) and to the right of that Roger Williams (1603–1684) Oliver Cromwell (1599–1658) and Stephen Bocskai (557–1606), Along the wall, to either side of the central statues is engraved the motto of both the Reformation _and_ of Geneva: _Post Tenebras Lux_ (Latin) After darkness light. The monument was created by two French sculptors: Paul Landowski and Henri Bouchard, and inspired one of the most important 20th century Hungarian poems written by Gyula Illyes under the title: The monument of Reformation in Geneva. It is an impressive sight visited by thousands every year and stands as a witness for Christ the Savior in the city which is the home of the UN.

HUGUENOTS (554)

Huguenots meaning "*United Together*" were members of the French Protestant Reformed church, inspired by the writings of John Calvin. Origin of the word is not known, what *is* known is that they believed the Bible is Gods Holy Word, and the Roman Church needed radical cleansing. Popes, Bishops and Priests were running a worldly kingdom, mocking the laws of God while exercising a great deal of control over kings & emperors, the clergy owned half of all the real estate in France, as well as other European countries. Those who protested were called Protestants and had grown rapidly to two million, (not just among the peasants), but primarily in circles of Intelligentsia & French Nobles. They wanted to guide the church back to its moorings; therefore Bishops and Priests saw Huguenots as a threat to their luxurious lifestyle and together with the help of the ever scheming mother of King Charles IX made a plan to get rid of all Huguenots in one day. The queen mother devised a plot and told the young king to invite all protestant nobles to the city for the wedding of the king's sister, and then kill them while they sleep. The king liked his mother's idea and a careful record was made of their stay; all the houses were marked, the church bells were the signal, and lights were installed at the highest points in Paris. Guards were dressed in white linen with the cross of Christ on their caps and a picture of the Virgin Mary around their neck. On the night of August 24, 1572 the young king was restless, thinking he should change his mind, but at midnight his mother entered the bedroom, led him to the window, and convinced him that he was doing the right thing, <u>it was the will of God</u>. Then gunfire reverberated through the city and bodies were thrown in the street. The Queen mother & the princess yelled courage my friends u have a great beginning. The king then closed his conscience, went in to the streets and took part in the blood-thirsty massacre. That night 70,000 Huguenots were murdered. When the news reached Pope Gregory, he & his cardinals led a procession and danced in the streets, blood continued to flow throughout France, women & children were killed in large numbers and filled the rivers with decaying bodies, so much so that wolves came down from the hills to feed upon carcasses. Those who participated in the St Bartholomew massacre were awarded the property of the person they killed. After that night, the king's conscience haunted him & king Charles of France became depressed; he contracted tuberculosis, his cough turned to blood, and he died in the most horrendous pain at age 24. Whether evil is done in the name of Allah or Christ, it is clearly Satanic. The St Bartholomew massacre of 1572 may have been, (along with the crusades a few centuries earlier), <u>the</u> darkest chapters in church history.

REFORMATION DAY
OCTOBER 31 (555)

Reforming of the church may have begun before, or at least with, the life of John Wycliffe, who was born in 1320. He was a scholar and stirred up major controversy in England about the corruption among the clergy. There was no separation of church & state, the church *was* the state. Jan Hus was born in 1371 in Bohemia (later called Czechoslovakia), he was a religious thinker and key predecessor of the 16th Century Protestant Reformation movement; he questioned the clergy and *for that* was burned at the stake in 1415 in Prague. He died singing Jesus son of David have mercy on me. Later a tall statue of him was erected in the center of Prague. William Tyndale was born in 1492; for *his crime of translating the Bible*, he was betrayed by an unprincipled friend, and burned at the stake in Belgium in 1536. Reforming the church was Gods work and was beginning to gain momentum at that time. Swiss born Ulrich Zwingli attempted to reform the church with the sword, and died on the battlefield in 1531. In 1509 John Calvin was born in Geneva and John Knox in 1513 in Scotland. All of these men made great contributions to reforming the church. Martinus Luder, (known at Martin Luther), at age 34, nailed his 95 theses, (*disagreements with the church*), to the Castle-Church-door of Wittenberg in Germany on Oct. 31, 1517; thus setting in motion what we know today as the Reformation. Later during the 1700's came the Brothers, John & Charles Wesley,

Jonathan Edwards, George Whitefield, and others. Historians have designated October 31 as Reformation Day. Martin Luther first studied law, but due to a conversion experience, he changed, and studied the Holy Scriptures receiving his doctorate of Bible and got a University teaching position. He was very proud of that degree and one time said: "*When Christ returns he will call & say: Doctor Luther come forth*." Luther was a product of the church, and by studying the Bible, his eyes were opened to all the distortions the church was teaching, and began exposing them. This got him excommunicated and became a hunted man. For Centuries the Roman Church kept the ordinary people illiterate, many (perhaps most), of the clergy were uneducated and had no knowledge of the Bible. Subsequently the church was plagued by superstition, ignorance, false doctrines, and corruption. It is now almost 600 yrs ago, that Luther took a bold stand for the truth. His action, and that of the Reformers have had a profound and lasting impact on the political, literary, artistic, and social as well as all aspects on modern society. The Reformation was at the heart of the Christian movement, it was the great breakthrough of the Gospel as the Good News of Salvation by grace through faith, and has become the greatest Re-Discovery in the history of mankind. Happy Reformation Day for October 31.

GREAT AMERICAN SEAL (469)

Before the Congress adjourned on July 4, 1776 three men, Dr Franklin, Mr. J. Adams, and Mr. Jefferson were charged with organizing a committee to design an emblem that would be a true reflection of the 56 brave men who helped to establish these 13 colonies in the New World and called it America, in such a way that it would reflect who we are. They eventually came up with the Great American Seal. The challenge was to translate principles & ideas into graphic symbols, and did so. Now whenever you see the president speak, he stands behind the Great Seal that represents the ideas and idealism of the founding fathers of our country in the stirring days of independence. Recommendations had been made to display the turkey, but I am happy the final choice was the bald eagle, which was chosen because of its great dignity and strength. In its wings it displays power of flight, meaning it is not earth bound, but has total freedom of the air. It is a bird of extraordinary vision, it can see a rabbit two miles away soar down at speeds of 100 mph; they were created to fly to great heights. The eagle is the only creature on land or sea which in a time of storm will not seek refuge in a cave or rock, it soars above the storm. They do not fly like other birds but sit on a high ledge and wait for the right currents, and effortlessly soar up to great heights. We chose this creature as the symbol of our nation to be a people of dignity, a nation of freedom and strength, not just military strength, but spiritual strength. The shield resting upon the breast of the eagle without any support, symbolizes that our country needs no outsiders to support us, but we stand on our virtues which is our foundation. In the eagle's right talon is an olive branch and in his left a bundle of 13 arrows. The tree colors of the flag are in the shield; White is for innocence and purity, Red for harvest and valor, and Blue is for justice, perseverance and vigilance. How can we show our virtues to the world unless they are found in our eyes? America is only as great as its people, and the leaders of this nation are its salesmen & women. E-PLUIRIBUS UNIM is Latin meaning from diverse backgrounds out of many one! One Nation under God. Over the head of the eagle the light has broken through the cloud and splits toward a constellation of 13 stars, representing the 13 colonies; the glory of the rays coming through the clouds symbolize the illumination of Almighty God upon our country, and reflects on the fact that we have taken our place among the nations of the world. In the harbor of New York stands the statue of Liberty symbolizing that we are the land of the free. I was at the June 4, 1989 student protest in Tiananmen Square and saw the students carry a replica of the statue of liberty protesting the China govt. policies; the world wants this liberty that we take for granted.

D-DAY 6 JUNE 1944 (557)

It was D-day of June 6, 1944 when order triumphed over evil with the invasion of Normandy which was the beginning of Adolph Hitler's defeat in Europe. The Atlantic undertaking involved 160,000 troops, 5,000 ships and 13,000 aircrafts, it remains the most complex strategy to this day as a testimony to a country, its allies and its people, that stood united based on dedication to duty and national pride with incredible courage and sacrifice against tyranny. Much was at stake for the whole world. President Franklin D. Roosevelt took the lead and prayed before the whole world in a prayer for faith in each other, so that liberty may be restored. He and his daughter Anna and family composed that prayer the night before. No one questioned the fact whether or not prayer was appropriate; the entire world stood with him while 160,000 men were attempting to conquer the steep cliffs of the French coast. All families were huddled in prayer for these young men (some as young as 16) that invaded Normandy. 9,000 lost their lives in that battle. Especially in Europe all families huddled in prayer hoping this may be the beginning of the end. The stakes were so high that boys too young to fight were lying about their age so they could serve; they understood the cause. At that time society was founded on faith, family, and unity; there was a strong will to sacrifice and help work for the common good to achieve victory. Western Europe, and America had a strong conviction of hierarchy and order, children respected their parents, teachers, and clergy as well as community leaders. It was not modern technology that won the great victory on D-day, but like minded people who gathered in churches and stood with their soldiers. Every porch hung a flag indicating support of a country that was united. There was not a beep out of the ACLU objecting to the public displays of prayer and troop support. Everyone understood what was needed, even atheists and unchurched individuals understood if we are to claim victory on this D-day there was a need to be united and stand together with one accord. Such unity became the turning point of Hitler's mighty war Machine. Instead of marching forward, battles were lost and the German soldiers were beginning to recognize that their efforts became futile against a force that was mightier then weapons. They faced the largest assault America had ever attempted anywhere. It became clear that in order to win we needed to speak with one voice. There was a national pride that had never been evident before. Even though the battle was on foreign soil the world marched as one nation under God and defeated the evil empire, D-day was costly but victorious.

SLAVERY (558)

This may come as a surprise to some of you but slavery was not invented in America, and neither do all slaves come from Africa; it has existed from the beginning days of the Old Testament in Biblical times, meaning it has been with us for thousands of years. From ancient times to the present day, the history of slavery spans different nationalities, ethnicities, cultures, and religions. It was practiced in Mesopotamia, which dates back to 3500 BC, and was practiced in all ancient civilizations, including the Roman Empire. It was somewhat less popular during the Early Middle Ages in Europe. Both Muslims & Christians captured and enslaved each other during the centuries of warfare in the Mediterranean nations. In the beginning of the 16th century, European merchants initiated the transatlantic slave trade and purchased Africans from West African kings & chiefs, who were eventually curtailed by European & American governments passing laws abolishing their nation's involvement. The dominant credits in England go to William Wilberforce, who while in Parliament led the anti slavery movement and succeeded in getting the Abolition Act signed in to law on 1 August 1833, two days after his death of 29 July, 1833. Abraham Lincoln in America who as president signed the emancipation act on 1 January 1863 and lived 2 years till he was assassinated on 14 April 1865. Today slavery is not legal anywhere in the world, but human trafficking remains a major international problem. Experts, who study this, have estimated 25-40 million people were enslaved as of 2013, with the majority of these being in Asia. Evidence emerged in the late 1990's of systematic child slavery and human trafficking in West Africa. It's estimated that slavery in the 21st century generates $150 billion in annual profits. Populations in regions with armed conflicts are especially vulnerable and modern transportation has made human trafficking easier. In 2019 there were an estimated 40 million people worldwide subject to some form of slavery, 25% were children. 61% are used in forced labor, mostly in the private sector; 38% live in forced marriages. For unknown reasons the Southern border of the US was opened wide and human smugglers known as Coyotes who charge up to $15,000 per migrant to bring them thousands of miles through Central America. Once the fee has been paid the coyotes own them until they cross the border where they are released in scorching scrubland where rattlesnakes and actual coyotes roam, if they survive, the women often end up in one form or another into sexual slavery far from what they were promised in their homeland where many lived under oppressive regimes. Will the US always be the land of the free?

STATUE OF LIBERTY (559)

The Statue of Liberty stands from ground level to torch 305 feet (93 meters) high on Liberty Island in New York Harbor and was designed by French Sculptor Frederic Auguste Bartholdi; it has become an icon of freedom and a symbol of welcome to immigrants arriving by sea. The Statue holds a torch above her head in her the right hand and in the left hand carries a tabula ensata inscribed in Roman numerals _July 4, 1776, (date of the Declaration of Independence_; a broken chain and shackle lay at her feet, commemorating the abolition of slavery following the American Civil War, which ended in 1865. Publisher Joseph Pulitzer started a drive for donations to finish the project which attracted more then 120.000 contributors, each giving less then a dollar, (_equivalent to $33 in 2022_). The statue was built in France, shipped in crates and assembled in New York Harbor; its completion marked by New York's first ticker-tape parade, and a dedication ceremony presided over by President Grover Cleveland on 28 Oct.1886. It has been maintained by the National Park Service and is a major tourist attraction, now attracting 10,000 visitors a day, 4.5 million a year, producing revenue of $263 million annually, that included us, having climbed that colossal statue to the very top, we are in awe, of the creation as well as the meaning of the artwork of early American history, two female figures as cultural symbols of the nation Marianne and Columbia. Marianne came to represent France and Columbia the traditional supplanted European personification of the

Americas as an Indian Princess. The statue has become a major landmark and is a "must see" for any tourist visiting New York. In 1982 President Ronald Reagan announced a major renovation project to be led by Chrysler Corporation Chair Lee Iacocca who raised the funds needed to complete the work, $350 million for the renovations of the Statue of Liberty as well as an upgrade of Ellis Island. From 1984 to 1986 the park was closed. Following renovation it was re-opened to the public, with a modern elevator installed. French President Francois Mitterrand came in person and attended the ceremony. Following the September 11 attacks in 2001 the statue was closed but reopened at the end of that year. It contains the tablet that bears the text of Emma Lazarus's sonnet, "The new Colossus" (1883), mounted inside the pedestal; a tablet declares the statue is a gift from the People of France honoring the Alliance of the two nations. A replica of the Statue of Liberty stands in Tokyo bay Japan. We were is China during the Tiananmen Square student protest in July 1976 and were surprised to see the students carrying a replica of the Statue of Liberty lifting it high in front of the picture of Mao Zedong, indicating a hunger for freedom; our guide advised us to leave the country during the turmoil it was a good feeling to see the statue of Liberty.

SILENT GENERATION (560)

Who are the people of the _silent generation_? We are told it refers to the people who are born in the 1930's and 40's; that really got our attention and reminded us of the great scholar called "Pogo" who said: "We found the enemy and it's us." According to Time Magazine the Silent Generation are mostly, (not all), immigrants who primarily focused on their careers rather then activism. They made the best of bad situations; among them were civil rights leaders, who lived with financial insecurity. In that group were industrial giants like Henry Ford, Lee Iacocca, Henry J Kaiser, Walt Disney, Marten Luther King, Margaret Thatcher, Mikhail Gorbachev, Dick Cheney, as well as Mary Tyler Moore, Clint Eastwood, Chuck Norris, Don Rickles and Johnny Carson. We are the generation who questioned Nancy Pelosi, when she introduced the Health Care bill, coined as Obama Care and said: "You have to pass it before you know what's in it", (in other words), _we legislators, who never worked in the private sector know what's good for you_. Many of us left families behind who lived under Fascism, Socialism, or Communism and were prepared to take risk. We came to the Land of Abe Lincoln who said in his Gettysburg address about _Government of the people, by the people, and for the people_, which he may have borrowed from One of Great Britain's early Reformers John Wycliffe who wrote in the prologue of his translation of the Bible, "_This Bible is for the government of the people by the people and for the people_". It was the driving force of the silent generation that made America the industrial giant it became among the nations of the world. We chose risk over security and those of us who came from foreign shores knew there is always risk attached to opportunity. We learned about the founding documents that said: we have certain unalienable rights one of which was _not_ Happiness but _the pursuit of_ Happiness, we chose risk & pioneering over security, and for most of us that meant 14 hour workdays six or seven days a week with no benefits, few or no vacations. We had already left behind affordable care which in the US has been a fraud, it never was affordable. It's indicative that our country made a u-turn back to the failed policies many of us tried to get away from. There was no childcare, when mom needed to see a specialist it meant 3 of the youngest children came on the bus to the city to be there by 9 am. We waited in freezing cold till the door opened and stayed in the full waiting room; at 5 pm the nurse announced those of u still waiting, come back tomorrow; that was _real_ affordable care, _free_. It is why we, the Silent Generation, have never shied away from hard work, took risk, all of which paved the way to the most successful experiment ever undertaken by mankind. We who belong to that group take pride in being coined the Silent Generation.

BREXIT (561)

The inner six European countries, (*Belgium, France, Germany, Italy, Luxembourg, and the Netherlands*), signed the Treaty of Paris in 1951 establishing the European Coal & Steel Community (ECSL). The UK attempted to join in 1963 and in 1967 but applications were vetoed by the president of France, <u>Charles de Gaulle</u>, who feared the UK would be a Trojan horse for US influence. De Gaulle resigned in 1969, and the UK successfully applied for membership in the European Communities (EC). In addition to the <u>inner six</u>, later the <u>outer seven</u> came on, (*Austria, United Kingdom, Denmark, Norway, Portugal, Sweden, & Switzerland*), all were added later. Membership of the then EEC was thoroughly discussed with long debates at the House of Commons in 1971, leading to a vote of 356 to 244 in favor. Prime Minister Edward Heath signed the Treaty of Accession in 1972. During the 1970s and 1980s skepticism surfaced in England, and support for membership in the EU never scored much above 5 or 6 % in Britain. Brexit was the withdrawal (British Exit) of the United Kingdom (UK) from the European Union (EU) on 1 February 2020. Up to this point the UK is the only sovereign country that has done so. The EU and its institutions developed gradually since their establishment. Throughout the period of British membership Eurosceptic groups have existed opposing aspects of the EU. Labor Prime Minister Harold Wilson held a referendum on its continued membership in 1975 in which 67% voted to stay; again a vote was held in 2016, even though the Brexit supporters did not win at that time, but ultimately persistency paid off and the Brexit supporters were victorious and voted to pull Great Britain out of the EU. Some economists claim that the action will hurt the UK. The withdrawal had been advocated by hard Eurosceptics for some time, with both sides of the arguments spanning the political spectrum. When in 1973 the UK joined the European Communities (EC), membership was endorsed in the 1975 referendum. In the 1970's and the 1980's withdrawal from the EC was advocated primarily by the political left more specifically in the Labor Party. On 29 March 2017, the British government formally began the withdrawal process by invoking article 50 of the treaty on European Union with permission from Parliament. It has been a long rigorous road but on 31 January 2020, the UK left the European Union. Its membership has been a contentious issue for the entire time that Britain has been a member. The nation was divided, meaning whether you do, or don't, half the people will disagree. Such divisive issues are tough on politicians who must lead and make choices; it is why political office should never be a popularity contest.

DELTA WORKS (562)

On Saturday 31 January 1953 dad took a few of us out of bed in the middle of the night and told us we are going to walk to the dyke; according to the Hilversum radio the storm surge, might brake some levies which could create serious floods. Our land is situated about 18 ft below sea level that meant extra pressure on the dyke, but the sea had never even reached the foot of the dyke and our home was about 1 mile in, therefore we should be safe, but mom was confined to bed with MS. The earthen dyke was sloping so we could walk up to the top and did so. _The site has never left my mind_. As we reached the top (likely about 24 ft above sea-level), there on the other side of the dyke was the ocean, just 1 foot away from us with water flopping over the dyke. Further south at 3 AM on 1 Feb. the Zeeland dykes breached in 67 locations and a large part of the land was inundated; there were 2551 deaths, 200,000 animals died and 3,500 houses and farms were lost. In the North-sea more then 230 deaths occurred on sea crafts along the Northern European Coast between Norway and Scotland. Ferries, Steamers, and Fishing- Trawlers sank, telephone lines were disrupted, and governments were ill prepared, emergency offices were not staffed, amateur radio operators went into the areas with their equipment. Relief money, food and blankets came in from England, Canada, USA, and other countries. Floods and dam breeches had occurred for centuries but never at the magnitude of the 1953 north-sea disaster. It set in motion a group of students, professors, engineers, and business people like never before aiming at solutions, fully realizing that due to indecision _and_ the second World War little action had been taken. It was the wake-up call. The Delta Works Commission was installed and studied damming, shortening coastlines, fewer dykes, (_Unlike the Zuidersea, where its purpose had been largely for land reclamation_); the Delta Plan was only defensive and required collaboration between National and Provincial authorities; it consisted of blocking the estuary mouths of 3 inlets and reduced the dykes exposed to the sea by 700 km (430 mi); the mouths of the new waterways were to remain open because of important shipping routes to the ports of Rotterdam and Antwerp. At the province of South Holland a _Dyke Ring_, was installed. Chances of a significant flood were calculated by models; for the purpose of the model a human life was valued at 2, 2 million Euros. In 1997 the work was done, fully completed and called The Delta Plan with sluices, locks, dykes, levees and storm surge barriers located in the provinces of South Holland and Zeeland completed with new roads and infrastructures. The American Society of Civil Engineers declared it one of the _Seven Wonders of the Modern World_.

UKRAINE WAR; IS THERE AN END? (564)

The 1991 dissolution of the Soviet Union has been a setback for Vladimir Putin, especially with the decline of the Russian fleet, about one fourth of which is parked at Crimea in the Black Sea; the most Eastern of the 24 Ukraine provinces. Its population is mostly Russian, Vladimir Putin falsely accused the Ukrainian government of committing racial atrocities against its Russian-speaking minority people and on 24 February 2022 he ordered a full scale invasion to re-capture Ukraine. We can not read Putin's mind. Being a former Lieutenant-Colonel in the KGB where he served for 16 years, may have miscalculated and assumed the country did not have an experienced leader, and it should be a simple process to take Ukraine back. Before Zelensky was elected President of Ukraine he was a comedian and TV star, therefore should be an easy pushover for a trained KGB agent like Putin who was Zelinsky's senior by 26 years. But the people of Ukraine rallied behind their new leader and he turned out to be much tougher then what you might expect from a comedy TV star. In Russia Vladimir Putin had succeeded Boris Yeltsin as Prime Minister, but things had not been a *shoe in*. Russia is characterized by an endemic of wickedness, jailing & repression of political opponents, violation of human rights and fixed elections politicized by a corrupt media. Since the war began thousands have died in Ukraine, towns & cities such as Mariupol lie in ruins and 13 million people have been displaced. Women & children occupy what is left of such towns while the men have been conscripted to fight the war with Russia. Vladimir Putin has refused to call it an invasion but continues to coin it a special military operation. The international community, including the US and Canada, have called Russia's invasion of Ukraine a Genocide. The words of Russia's leaders now ring very hollow when they claim: "It is not our plan to occupy the Ukrainian territory; we do not intend to impose force." Andrei Kortunov, head of the Russian International Affairs Council said: Putin needs success, or at least requires something he can present to his constituency at home to show a victory, we might call that: *He needs to save face*', which is a core social value most prevalent in Asian cultures. Putin, after he became prime minister, signed into law constitutional amendments allowing to potentially extend his presidency to 2036 or his age 84, meaning he is president for life, which is the dream of most politicians. There you have it: Putin needs to win and wants to annex Ukraine, Ukraine wants to be free from oppression and enjoy independence; they have tasted Western life since 1991 and are ready to go back; Putin has only known oppression & domination; a peaceful solution requires the Wisdom of Solomon.

KEYSTONE XL PIPELINE (565)

Keystone XL Pipeline is the $8 billion 2,687 mile (4,324 km) long pipeline to bring oil to the US from our Canadian neighbor & ally, rather than keep depending on the Middle Eastern nations who would rather see us cease & desist. The offer came in from TC Energy, formerly _Trans Canada pipeline Ltd_ to solve the problem of high gas prices; it would connect heavy crude oil from deposits in Canada to South Eastern refining networks in the United States. It has been controversial for many years due to concerns about its local and global environmental impacts. These issues have never been a problem for us here in Hawaii. In March 2019, then-president Donald Trump, granted a Presidential Permit allowing construction of the oil pipeline that was to run through the international border of the United States and Canada. However on January 20, 2021, President Biden signed an executive order revoking the permit of the Keystone XL pipeline. It was first proposed by Trans-Canada Corp on February 9, 2005 who said we are in the business of connecting energy supplies to markets and we view this opportunity as another way of providing a valuable service to our customers; converting one of our natural gas pipeline assets for oil transportation is an innovative, cost competitive way to meet the need for pipeline expansions to accommodate anticipated growth in Canadian crude oil production during the next decade. The pipeline goes from Hardisty, Alberta, to Steele city. Nebraska, and on to Wood River Refinery in Roxana, Illinois and the Patoka Oil Terminal Hub north of Patoka, Illinois. Section 2 runs from Nebraska through Kansas to the tank farm in Cushing Oklahoma, then further south to Texas refineries. The 3rd phase is the Houston lateral pipeline in Liberty county Texas to refineries and terminates in the Houston area. Why is there a concern? In October 2019 there was a spill of 378,000 gallons in North Dakota. Our Hawaii Reps in Washington have consistently opposed the pipeline. Schatz even went out of his way to enlist support in Congress to make sure that we remain dependent on the Middle East. At election time, we have known for years that Hawaii only votes for Democrats. In the past we were asking why not vote for a person rather then vote blindly for a party and do you know how these people vote? The answer was always the same, _we do not know_ & _we do not care_; _we only want Democrats to represent us_. Filling up my gas tank is beginning to hurt. In the 1950's we bought the best product for the car, but now we feel compelled to change to the cheaper product & buy the regular gas. Our Canadian neighbors have some three million miles of oil & gas pipelines, mostly in the wilderness, so why do we go to the Middle East and not to our Northern neighbors?

KENNEDY / LINCOLN (566)

Are the Kennedy/Lincoln similarities just coincidences, or are they real? Here are some: * Lincoln & Kennedy each have 7 letters; *Both were elected to Congress in "46, Lincoln representing Illinois was elected in 1846, & Kennedy representing Massachusetts was elected in 1946; *Both men were elected to the presidency in '60, Lincoln became president in 1860, & Kennedy in 1960, Both men had serious concerns about civil rights, Lincoln wanted freedom for slaves & signed the Emancipation Act. Kennedy wanted racial equality. Both were married in their 30's to women in their 20's, Lincoln married Mary Anne Todd at his age 33 when she was 23; Kennedy married Jacqueline at his age 36 when she was 24. Both were assassinated by a Southerner on Friday; Lincoln was shot in the head on Good Friday Apr. 14, 1865 by John Wilkes Booth from Maryland. Kennedy was shot in the head by Lee Harney Oswald from New Orleans on Friday Nov. 22, 1963; both were succeeded by Southern vice presidents named Johnson; Lincoln was succeeded by Andrew Johnson from Tennessee, and Kennedy by Lyndon Baines Johnson from Texas. Both assassins were known by 3 names. Lincoln's killer was John Wilkes Booth and the assassin of Kennedy was Lee Harvey Oswald. Each had names composed of 15 letters, Lincoln was shot in Ford Theater, and Kennedy was riding while he was shot in a Ford Lincoln. Both assassins died before they were put on trial. Booth was chased but refused to surrender, and was killed by sergeant Boston Corbett on April 26, 1865.

Lee Harvey Oswald was assassinated on November 24, 1963 by night club owner Jack Ruby. There are quite a few other stories floating around but we were not able to verify them. Lincoln had a secretary called Kennedy and Kennedy had a secretary called Lincoln. We could not verify that. Then there is the one that Booth ran from the theater and was caught in a warehouse. And Lee Harvey Oswald ran from a warehouse and was caught in the theatre. As far as we can determine that is incorrect. The list of coincidences appeared in the mainstream American press in 1964 one year after the assassination of President Kennedy in Dallas Texas. Other comparisons of world leaders have not similarities but are more extreme opposites such as: Hitler & Lee Kuan Yew. We have experienced both. Hitler changed Europe from going forward to near total destruction. And Lee Kuan Yew changed Singapore from a failing third world country to the most advanced city in the world, a 20th century showcase. We stopped in Singapore in 1957 and again a few years ago, and he has given us an East Asian perspective that exceeds any imagination; our linguistic ability is inadequate to describe the new Singapore, changed into a world class city.

FORGIVE A (567)

Rev. Billy Kim, (who was translator for Billy Graham in Korea) stopped for a rest in our home on his way to Chicago and shared this story: "From 1910 to 1945 Korea was occupied by Japan. Missionaries were ordered to leave; churches were closed and told to worship at Shinto Shrines. The Japanese commander told the pastor of a small Korean Church; You may have one service next Sunday, after that no more. People walked as far as 12 miles just to worship one more time. In church while the people sang the hymn: "_Alas & did my Savior bleed_", the troops pored kerosene around the church, set it on fire, and were told shoot & kill anyone getting out. None did, all died. Question: Should the children and family members forgive? Years later, Christians from Japan visited Korea and learned about that. Went back to Japan, raised money, returned to Korea and built a new community center, church, and medical clinic; during the dedication ceremony the Koreans embraced the Japanese they had forgiven. _The Seattle Times_ carried this ad: _two year old Porsche for sale $500_. A man responded and said: Lady, to be honest this is a $60,000 car what is wrong with it? She said _nothing_! My husband left with a neighbor-girl, he called and said: "I am not coming back, sell the car, and sent me the money; I am doing as he asked." We do not like to admit that hate rages below the surface, but hate needs healing. (Professor Lewis Smedes, (was a friend, fell of a ladder and died in Dec. 2002), When in Hawaii he shared this: German General Herman Engel at the Nuremburg trail was sentenced to

30 years for atrocities; he and his soldiers had massacred an entire town including all of Morreiaux family. Engel survived the 30 years and purchased a cabin in the woods. He and his wife hoped to live out their life in peace incognito forgotten by the world. Morreiaux (a French journalist) recognized him, had privately condemned him to death, he stoked up the fanatics in the village hoping to do what the Nuremburg court had not done. It was the village revenge, but something bothered him; he wanted to get to Engel first, climbed the hill and introduced himself to the now visibly shaken, unsuspecting Engle, spent the afternoon grilling him about the village massacre. Engel's feeble humanity seemed more like a tired old man, <u>not the monster that had lived in his mind for 30 years</u>, giving Morreiaux doubt; his vengeance was now contaminated, and blurted out: the villagers will come and kill u tonight; he offered to lead him to safety. But Engel said: "<u>*I'll go with you on one condition, that u forgive me*</u>". Morreiaux already had condemned him 1000 times and could no longer be the person he was, <u>without</u> the hatred, he <u>belonged</u> to his hate; Forgiveness was the only thing that could set him free, and he could not do it. When you forgive u heal yourself, and set the prisoner free, discovering you were that prisoner.

FORGIVE B (568)

Simon Wiesenthal, a Jew who survived Auschwitz shared this: During his concentration camp internment a nurse came and led him to the bedside of one of Hitler's most savage forces, a young 19 yr old SS Soldier. His head wrapped in yellow pus-stained bandages. The boy was dying and said: I called for u, I need to speak to a Jew. He could barely breathe, & said: "We were fighting in a Russian village, rounded up 200 Jews, crammed them like sardines in a house, and then threw grenades through the windows, the house burned. On the 2nd floor was a man, with a baby in his arms, his free hand covered the child's face, next to him a lady, may be his wife. He saw me, as our eyes locked, he jumped, and so did the lady, and we shot them. That face is with me day & night, it haunts me; (he paused struggling for breath), and said I know this is hard for you but I need forgiveness from a Jew or I can not die in peace. As the afternoon sun-rays fell through the window of that dismal hospital room, there were 2 strangers, caught up in the crisis of forgiveness: One of the Super Race the NAZIS, begging forgiveness from a member of the condemned race a Jew. There was eerie-silence, and without another word Wiesenthal stood up and left the room, the young soldier went to God as his judge, unforgiven by men. Wiesenthal survived that camp, but his actions troubled him. He ended his book: _The Sunflower_ with this steely question: _What would you have done?_ Before you answer, think of this: Wiesenthal was a successful Austrian Architect-Engineer, was dragged out of his home in the night, business was confiscated, spent 4 years in that concentration camp where he was starved, and tortured! _That is not all_, the NAZIS murdered 89 of his relatives in gas-ovens; what should you do? Just get over it? Vengeance is a hot desire to get even and give back the pain someone gave you, but it never gets what it wants. Refuse to forgive is like taking a cup of poison & drink it yourself; it never evens the score, fairness never comes. Forgiving heals memory. Wiesenthal died in Vienna on 20 Sept, 2005 at age 96. He was never a free man. In the Passover Exodus 12 God led His people to freedom, what had to be remembered??? 400 yrs of captivity? No!! _The freedom, the release, the liberation, the redemption_, not the bondage. not the wrongs. He says in Matthew 6:15? _If you do not forgive, your Father will not forgive you_. Corrie Ten Boom spent 5 days in our home, she lost her sister and father in one of those concentration camps, she said when God forgives he changes his memory. After you forgive someone, you begin to see a deeper truth about them, a truth that our hate blinds us too. God takes your wrongs and casts them in the deepest ocean. Then places a sign there that says: NO FISHING ALLOWED.

MOTHER'S DAY (569)

Happy Mothers day, which may have begun in America in 1905, but my vote, goes to Hannah listed in 1 Samuel 1 in the Holy Bible. If it was not for the modern day items like dryers, TV, and others that chapter could have been about my mother. I read a mother's day essay, can't remember where may be in _Dear Abby_ or _Ann Landers_ forgive me if this is wrong, but here is: Mother's Day. "Mom and Dad were watching TV when mom said, I'm tired it's getting late, I think I'll go to bed. She got up and went to the kitchen to make sandwiches for the next day's lunches, rinsed the popcorn bowls, took meet out of the freezer for supper the following evening, checked the cereal box levels, filled the sugar container, put spoons and bowls on the table set up the coffee pot for brewing the next morning, take the wet clothes of the floor, put them in the dryer, sewed up a loose button, picked up the newspapers that were strewn on the floor and the game pieces left on the table, put the phone book back in the drawer. She watered the plants, emptied the wastepaper basket, hung up a towel to dry wrote a note to the teacher put some cash in an envelope for the children's field trip. Addressed and stamped the birthday card for Abby's friend, put water in the dog dish opened the door for the cat to go outside, made sure all the doors are locked, window are closed, as she was ready to wash her face, when dad called: _I thought you were going to bed an hour ago, I fell asleep, just woke up and you are still not here, how is it that you are always so slow_, while adding a few items to the grocery list for tomorrow, and write a note for dad, don't forget to change your left front tire before u go, I noticed it is flat. Finally she is ready for bed, looked in on each of the children, specially Suzie who had complained about ear ache, put the carton of milk back in the refrigerator, and notices dad is fast asleep, sets the alarm for 3 AM to check on Suzie's ear ache. The next morning Max's sister stops in for coffee and says I have a perfect job for you, Max should not have to carry the load here alone." Happy Mother's day! Here is one more. "Amanda age 5 says: Mommy how come all your hair is black and three of them are white, happy for the question she seizes the opportunity for a teaching moment, but sometimes it is better to plan such moments in advance, here was her answer: When you are a bad girl, rather then get angry and spank you, mom worries about you and one hair turns white. Amanda was happy with that answer, but she returned a few minutes later and said: Mommy all of grandma's hair is white that means you must have been a very bad girl. Be careful what you tell your children specially if they are half as smart as you are. _Happy mothers day_; we suggest reading _Proverbs 31_, especially the epilogue, the last 21 verses, there is great wisdom in there for all of us.

FATHERS DAY (570)

Tribute <u>too</u> and praises <u>for</u> fathers. <u>4</u> <u>Years old</u>: My daddy can do anything he is stronger then all the daddies of my friends. <u>7 years old</u> my dad knows more then all the teachers in the whole school he knows a lot because he is very smart. <u>9 years old</u> my father does not know everything <u>12 years old</u> My father knows nothing about that, they did not know much, when he was in school he is from another universe, it was a time that not much was known yet <u>14 years old</u> Dad is old fashioned he would not understand, he is hopelessly out of date, what did you expect from an old man <u>21 years old</u> Dad is behind the time he has been out of school a long time and most things were invented later <u>25 years old</u> Dad knows a little about it but today we know so much more he did not keep up <u>30 years</u> old that's interesting, I wonder what dad thinks about that lets ask him <u>35 years old</u> Before we proceed lets get dad's perspective on that, I wonder what he would think about that <u>40 years old</u> I don't want to do anything on that until I hear from dad he might do it completely different, he most likely tried it <u>45 years old</u> Dad was pretty smart he taught us to look at it from anther angle <u>50 years old</u> Dad made us see things we did not see he had more experience <u>60 years old</u> We are still learning but dad knew exactly what to do, there was nothing he did not think of <u>65 years old</u> I'd give anything if dad was here he thought of things no one had even dreamed off dad had wisdom no one thinks like him its sad they don't make m like my dad any more they broke the mold, never met anyone like him, he was a grand old man, he had more wisdom in his fingers than most people have in their head he knew the answers.

The first father's day in America was celebrated in 1910. Since then Fathers day has been celebrated on the third Sunday in June. The state of Washington was the first state to celebrate the Holiday and America now spends an average of One billion dollars on presents. On one hand more & more children grow up without a dad, but on the other hand, fathers who are involved and become more active in their children's lives. Pew Research Center reports show that children raised without a father are at higher risk of behavioral problems, are more likely to be incarcerated in their lifetime, twice as likely to never graduate from high school, at seven times higher risk of teen pregnancy, more likely to abuse drugs and alcohol. My dad was financially poor, but supported seven children, could not help much mom was sick but we had a happy family and dad was always there when he could be there, he was available, and all siblings turned out (not rich) but did well and are independent. He taught us how to respect our leaders, even when they are wrong. Grades are forgotten but action is remembered.

DOLLAR BILL (571)

Have you ever taken the time to look at a one dollar bill? Silver certificates were issued between 1878 and 1964 in the United States as part of its circulation of paper currency. The Coinage Act of 1873 created by Alexander Hamilton stopped production of silver dollars, and people began to refer to the passage as the crime of 1873. It was not till three fourth century later that the *"so called"* paper money came of the presses first in 1957 in its present design. It is called paper money, but is in fact a cotton and linen blend; we have all washed it without falling apart; a special blend of ink is used the contents of that we will never know. It is overprinted with symbols, then starched to make it water resistant and pressed to give it that nice crisp look. The current design of the United States one dollar bill dates back to the early 1960's when the bill became a Federal Reserve note as opposed to a Silver Certificate, many of the design elements had been established over 30 years earlier. The treasury seal and serial numbers were dark blue, (now the color is green); under Washington's portrait the words One Dollar. In 1963 the one dollar bill began using its new treasury seal with English words instead of Latin. The World War II years featured several special printings including the Hawaii overprints; the Government was concerned that Hawaii might be lost to the Japanese and wanted to be able to devalue the money should this invasion occur. The Japanese invasion did not occur but a serious attack did on 7 December 1941, with the bombing of Pearl Harbor. In 1957 the $1 bill became the first US currency to bear the motto _In God we trust._ The Federal Reserve estimates the lifetime of a $1 bill to be about 4.8 years, and a $5 bill to be about 3.8 years, a $10 bill is estimated to live 3.6 years. There are 14 billion $1 bills in circulation. When bills become too old and worn out, they are taken out of circulation and are shredded by the Federal Reserve. They sometimes sell shredded bills to companies that use them in building materials, recycled currency may be in the shingles on your roof, or the insulation in the walls of your home, meaning that our house might have been made of money after all. Occasionally you may see redesigns of other currency; it's not likely that the $1 bill will get a makeover any time soon. The face on the $1 bill has been that of George Washington since 1869. The back of the one dollar bill features the bald Eagle and if Franklin had gotten his way we'd be seeing the turkey there. He found the Eagle a bird of bad moral character, and would not be a good icon for a great nation, because it was not responsible enough to do its own fishing, and thought the turkey would be a more suitable choice and described it as a more respectable bird and a true original native of America, and should be a more true representative of who we really are.

SOCIAL SECURITY (572)

When the pioneers came to the New World they wanted opportunity not security and were willing to take risk. Social Security was started as an old age survivor & disability Act and signed into law on April 5, 1935 by President Franklin D. Roosevelt (FDR) with the promise that you would only pay 1% of the first $1,400 of your wages and it would never be raised. Republicans voted against it but Democrats favor the Nanny-State idea and voted for it. The plan was voluntary and the contribution was tax deductible, it is now 6. 2 % and 6. 2 % is contributed by the employer, and it's <u>not</u> voluntary, <u>nor</u> is it tax deductible, and if you die before retiring your designated beneficiary gets $255, and all funds u paid in to the program belongs to the government. If Social Security was privatized, like your SEP, Pension Plans, IRA's, TSA's, Keogh's and other retirement plans, the funds in there will be paid to you at a certain age; in the event of death, it will go to your designated beneficiary; that is <u>not</u> so with Social Security, even though you have contributed all the funds in to the plan and it should belong to you, or your estate. In 2005 Republican President George Bush outlined a major initiative to Reform Social Security which included partial privatization of the system; he campaigned for it by going on a 60 day national tour; but in 2006 Democrats got control and killed the plan. After age 62 you can receive a slightly reduced life income, although it's better to wait till age 65. Congress excluded House & Senate members and installed a much more lucrative plan for their own retirement. But with much public pressure that changed in 1980 when elected officials were pressed to be in the same program as all of us regular folks. Up to that time: "*it was good for thee, but not for me*" When Terry was in the financial business, in one of the re-education classes we calculated our own Social Security, invested it at just 3% and were quite surprised to see the result was substantially higher then what Social Security was scheduled to pay us. Of course there are many variables such as widow's pension, children's benefit under age 18 to 22, but if you are a high wage earner and self incorporated, meaning you pay both your own and the employer's portion, and if *all* u wanted to do, was recover your own money which could have been invested conservative; our calculation indicated that in order to simply recover our own money one needed to live to about 150 years of age. We still believe that the original intend for the masses was a good idea even though there should have been an option out for the high wage earner. With regards to the concern that the fund will run out, we do *not* believe that our elected officials will let the program run dry, and will adjust it long before.

TRANSUBSTANTIATION (573)

Transubstantiation is a Latin word taught by the Catholic Church that the bread and wine of communion change into the body and blood of Christ. We learned about it so many years ago that I resolved never to use it again, and was sure I was the only person that would dream about such words, until a protestant friend walked in my office and flawlessly expressed it. The Catholic Church teaches: it is the change brought about in the Eucharistic prayer through the efficacy of the word of Christ and by the action of the Holy Spirit. The manner, in which it occurs, is a mystery and varies; for example, Augustine said: "Not all bread, but only that which receives the blessing of Christ becomes the body of Christ. Another example was the strange alliance of prominent and early reformer: Professor and Scholar John Wycliffe, (referred to as Morning Star), enjoyed a unique friendship with *John of Gaunt*, (Duke of Lancaster and third son of Edward III); it has been said that their friendship may have been causing the *palace revolution* in 1371, although there occurred a slight rift in their friendship when *John de Gaunt* discovered that one of Dr Wycliffe's contentions with the church was transubstantiation. I know the rift was serious, but am not certain *how* or if it affected their friendship, may be that is why I should never be called a historian but just a person who loves history. We know the term transubstantiation was used in the 11th century and was in widespread use by the 12th century during the Fourth Council of the Lateran in 1215; there the dispute was no matter how pious a layperson may be he should never hold leadership positions in the church, reverberation outlasted the century. It was a topic in the Council of Trent (split meeting spread over 18 years 1545 to 1563); mostly dealing with issues of the Reformation, such as this one. Martin Luther and Huldrych Zwingli heavily criticized it and referred to it as a pseudo philosophy; Luther devoted much of his book *The Babylonian Captivity* to that issue; in there he refers to Sacramental Union which may be erroneously called "*consubstantiation.*" We have always understood that Lutherans explicitly reject transubstantiation believing that the bread an wine remain fully bread and wine; having said that, in Luther's dialogue with Catholic theologians a large measure of agreement was reached. We did not feel competent to debate the issue with our Lutheran pastor Norman Pfotenhauwer here in Honolulu, but by agreement all the years we attended his Lutheran church, we abstained from communion. We believe Classical Presbyterianism is more in line with Calvin, who on such issues relied much on his friend Theodore Beza who was Calvin's pastor even preached his funeral sermon in May 1564. It is our understanding that the communion we practice today is Beza's teaching and is midway between Luther & Zwingli.

FLAG OF UNITED STATES (574)

The US Flag is the third oldest in the world. It was first authorized by Congress June 14, 1777; it required there be a star and stripe for each state. The date is observed as Flag Day throughout America. The colors are to be red for zeal and fervency; white for purity and hope and rectitude of conduct, blue the color of heaven and for reverence to God, for sincerity, justice and truth. The star symbolizes dominion, sovereignty, and Liberty. In 1818 Congress enacted that the number of stripes remain at 13 while a star should be added for each succeeding state. The US Flag is unique in the deep and noble significance of its message to the entire world, a message of national independence, of individual liberty, of idealism and patriotism. It is not the Flag of a reigning family or royal house, but of its millions of free people, welded into a nation, united not only by community of interest, but by vital unity of sentiment and purpose; a Nation distinguished for the clear individual conception of its citizens alike of their duties, their privileges, obligation and rights. It incarnates for all mankind the spirit of Liberty and the glorious ideal of human freedom of unrestrained Liberty but unique ideal of equal opportunity for life, liberty and the pursuit of happiness, safeguarded by the lofty principles of duty, righteousness and justice, attainable by obedience to self-imposed laws. Floating from the lofty pinnacle of American idealism; it is a beacon of enduring hope, it floats over a wondrous assemblage of people from every racial stock of the earth whose hearts constitute an indivisible force for the defense of the downtrodden. It embodies the essence of patriotism. Its spirit is the spirit of the American nation; its history is the history of the American peoples their fortunes and their sacred honor. Ever victorious, it has emerged triumphant from great national and international conflicts. It first rose over 13 states along the Atlantic seaboard with a population of 3 million people. President Woodrow Wilson issued a proclamation designating June 14 as Flag-day every year. In 1949 Truman signed an Act of Congress designating June 14 as Flag-day each year. Today it flies over 50 states across the continent from sea to sea. Citizens have advanced it and heroes have died for it, and let us always accord it with honor and loyalty. At our home we have a large 15 ft pole in the front yard and celebrate Flag-day every day. Coming out from living under Hitler I can think of no greater earthly blessing then living free and be able to fly the US Flag every day. We fail to understand why American Battle Monument Commission (ABMC) cancelled the traditional customary Boy & Girl Scout activity of placing a flag on all the graves of our National cemeteries. These twenty six American military cemeteries, most of them located on foreign soil, proving our commitment to the human race.

STAMP ACT 1765 (575)

The stamp Act, also known as, _Duties in American Colonies Act 1765_; was an Act of Parliament of Great Britain imposed to pay tax to the king of England on any printed materials in the colonies produced on stamped paper from London which included legal documents, magazines, playing cards, newspapers and many other types of paper used throughout the colonies, the tax had to be paid in British-Pounds, _(not in the currency that was in use at the time in the New World)_. The purpose of the tax was to pay for military troops that the king kept stationed in the American Colonies after the French and Indian War, but the colonists never feared a French invasion; therefore they contended that London should pay for their own troops. The Act had passed by a vote of 205–49 in the House of Commons and unanimously in the House of Lords. This allowed Britain to dispatch 10,000 troops to the American frontiers. John Adams wrote disparagingly of the deployment, as well as the revenue demanded from America "_To maintain swarms of officers and pensioners in idleness and luxury_". As would be expected the Stamp Act was not popular among the colonists, even more so, the Act was considered a violation, and protests were organized throughout the colonies. The colonists were for the most part former British citizens that had left their homeland to get away from English rules they found oppressive, wanting to be free of England, and begin a new life in the colonies, that was not all; there was no one from the colonies that represented them in Parliament. The slogan became: "*No taxation without representation*." Some assemblies sent petitions to Parliament and to the king expressing their strong opposition; such action was not limited to the colonies; raising taxes in Britain was out of the question especially after the virulent protests that had taken place in England earlier. Some responded to the King and said: We fled from your tyranny to an uncultured and unhospitable country we have been exposed to hardships, cruelties, and foes, and are jealous of our liberties, and refuse to pay the tax. Then went one step further; in protest they boycotted British products, which resulted in British merchants and manufacturers also putting the pressure on Parliament because their exports to the colonies were returned or refused; with this pressure on Parliament, the British had no choice, the Act was repealed a year later in 1766, but Parliament affirmed its power to legislate for the colonies, and past the Declaratory Act. A series of new taxes and regulations were imposed, all of which were opposed by the Americans, and led to the American Independence in 1776.

CONVENTION OF STATES (576)

Convention of States, what is it, and why do we need it? Our founding fathers were endowed with much wisdom, even though these men lived centuries ago, they predicted there would be a rise of big government, with tyrannical leaders who have no use for a constitution that advocates limited government. These pioneers left behind a tyrannical king and were fully aware of the fact that this could happen in the New World and being men of great learning they left us with a powerful tool right inside the Constitution such as article 5, which states in part: "*The Congress, whenever two thirds of both Houses shall deem it necessary, shall propose Amendments to this Constitution, or, on the application of the Legislatures of two thirds of the several States shall call a Convention for proposing Amendments.....as part of this Constitution when ratified by the Legislatures of three fourths of the several Sates.....Mode of ratification may be proposed by the Congress.....*" Our space is limited but the essence of it is here. By making use of this tool it will allow us to build a firewall against socialism, the very socialism that America is now headlong plunging into. By using this tool it should solidify our foundations of which the Congress, the White House, and the Courts, can not break. The founders feared a runaway government even though it seemed remote in 1776 they left us this tool. So who calls for this meeting, the President? No! The governors? No! Two third of State Legislatures, thereby returning the power to the States, exactly what Congress had in mind, not the Federal Government. *As a young boy I was intrigued by stories of ancient prairie fires, when all the animals stampeded and blindly plunged into the ravine*, I cried for the animals. Now the Media, the Democratic Party, and the Far Left are unstoppable with little clear thinking at the top; we are stampeding for the cliff; the time has come to invoke Article V of the US Constitution, if we do, should we re-write the entire constitution? *No*! Here are some as expressed by legal minds; **1**: Term limits for lawmakers, even look at, and revisit lifetime tenure of judges. **2**: Balance the Budget, model it after my family income, which is spent less than we earn; leaving our children a debt of $30 trillion is insane. **3**: Remove Education from DC and close that office, give it back to the parents, they did it successfully in New Zealand, fathers & mothers can decide what is good for their child, not some leftist bureaucrat in DC. **4**: Only legislative laws, no more executive orders, pontificating, from the top. We left the King in London. If it can't be approved by two Houses, it must not be good. Is this a movement? Yes! 19 states have already begun two thirds of fifty is doable.

YEAR OF THE CHILD (577)

The United Nations published this Declaration: "The Child's Rights" in 1959. It was a follow up to the _International year of the child_. When I was in Geneva, Hal Jones asked me to go with him to a meeting at the UN where this topic was on the agenda. The Declaration was lengthy, but here is item #10: "_The child shall be protected from practices which may foster religious or any other form of discrimination_." Wow, now it became clear why Hal had made me promise to keep my mouth shut, so I honored his request and said nothing; we were not there to participate but were invited to the meeting as observers. It was just as well because I would have asked about _any form of discrimination_. My attention span was short as we listened to a true feminist; I would have preferred to hear from anti Seike who raised 11 eleven children. We remained polite and left, I asked the lady at the door: Is she married? Answer: I don't know, she often comes with her lady friend. I much preferred this _true story_ of Timmy who was five or six years old. He said: Daddy how much money do u make in one hour? Timmy that is none of your business, but if you must know, I make $20 an hour, now go to bed it is getting late. Timmy went up asking can I borrow $10. Father got angry about such silly question and sent him to his room; Timmy went quietly upstairs. An hour later dad went up there thinking, may be I was too hard on him and better say sorry, but it was too late, Timmy was already asleep. Then something caught his eye, under the nightlight; there next to the bed was a piece of paper, an envelope and some crumpled up money, and an unfinished note said: Dear daddy it takes too long to get $20 but when I have $10 can I buy u for a half hour, I will ask Uncle Dale for some more next week. That true story says more then the UN can say in a year. Why are we searching the books and essays while the answers are in our homes; every morning we drove an hour or more to school and filled that with story time, taking turns in telling the story but I got out-voted most of the time; what they wanted was the war stories, and as they got a little older, corrected me saying it was this way not that way, a clear indication they had remembered. In addition to the car stories we also did weekend mountain hikes. On these they brought their friends, we went most Saturday mornings or Sunday afternoon after church to give mom a break. We limited these hikes to 10, if the group became 15, I asked another father. We only got lost once, but after a few hours found our way out of the woods. The children's ages varied from 7 to 12 only boys and one little 5 or 6 year old girl, (_my grand child_), chaperoned by her 2 year older brother. Do we need the UN with the high salaries and business suits? I prefer a real family with all its imperfections.

DEATH PENALTY (578)

Death Penalty or Capital Punishment; is it right? Or is it wrong? Is it justice? Or is it barbaric? Opponents argue it does not deter, it is my contention that it does; once a guilty person has been executed he can not repeat the crime, therefore it does deter. It should not be the primary reason for administering the death penalty, nor for that matter any other criminal penalty, although deterrence appears to be the primary issue on both sides. We contend that it would be both immoral and unjust to punish any person to scare others. The basic consideration for any punishment should always be: Is the punishment deserved, and does it fit the crime, meaning you should not be fined thousands of dollars for stealing a loaf of bread. If deterrence supersedes justice as the basis for criminal sanctions, then guilt or innocence becomes largely irrelevant; deterrence can be as effectively achieved by executing an innocent person. Intellectual honesty tells us that the effect is somewhat like the lighthouse, we do not know how many ships it has saved. Another argument is what if a mistake is made; execution is not reversible, of cause so is murder. If judges and juries can make wrong decisions, so can psychiatrists and parole boards. It has been argued that only the poor are executed, but by using that logic we should abolish prisons, the same holds for allegations that execution is legalized murder. By that definition one would have to conclude that arrest and imprisonment is nothing more then legalized kidnapping and legalized slavery. Lee Harvey Oswald assassinated President

Kennedy; Jack Ruby shot and killed Oswald, a convicted killer, *right or wrong*? We have laws; Ruby took the law into his own hands, and declared Oswald guilty, he was sentenced to death for that, but on appeal it was overturned, Ruby died of lung cancer while in prison waiting for his appeal. What does God require? Centuries before the complicated mosaic laws, God spelled out his requirement in Gen. 9:6: "*Whoever sheds the blood of men; by men shall his blood be shed*." Why? For God made men in his own image. The Lord has never rescinded that command, meaning murder is striking against God. What about forgiving? God in His holiness is not able to forgive without punishment. Forgiveness of wrong comes only by accepting the fact that Jesus paid the full price for our wrongs. Why was a brilliant lawyer like Chuck Colson opposed to the Death Penalty? I asked him, he was not. He said this: "We live in a fallen society where laws are not applied equally. In principle, based on Scripture, I am for the death penalty for murder, but we live in a world where laws are *not* applied equally, that means justice is not equal and Capital Punishment is final would then become unfair. (That was the essence of his reasoning).

PALMYRA ATOLL, MURDER MYSTERY (579)

In the summer of 1974 we were glued to the television after work every night watching the development of a mystery story on the evening news as it was happening; we had come out of New Zealand and the Palmyra story was unraveling about 1000 miles south of Hawaii in the direction of Tahiti. I was not much of a TV fan, actually was too busy establishing my financial business. But this story was real; we followed it daily blow by blow as it was developing. Vincent Bugliosi and Bruce Henderson wrote: "*And the sea will tell*", which may be helpful, but in this case the events are so vivid in our memory, I will rely on the reports of that time as conveyed. There may not have been many who followed it as close as we did, even went to the harbor and took pictures of the yacht. Mac and Muff Graham's 37 ft ketch was called the *Sea Wind* kept in immaculate condition stocked with supplies and had plans to visit Hawaii, Fiji, Palmyra, Tahiti and others; news-reports stated that his favorite was Palmyra lagoon. What was unique about them, instead of using tupperware or plastic on their yacht, they used fine china, crystal, and real silverware. They were people of class and there not being many other travelers in Palmyra, they met Walker & Stearns from Hawaii and befriended them, but for unknown reason Grahams no longer made contact, and friends assumed they enjoyed their retirement doing what they loved to do and that was exploring the South

Pacific. But a woman from Africa made a stop at Palmyra and discovered a chest in the water with bones, retrieved them, and had them analyzed, it was Muff Graham who had been a happily married lady. Friends had contact with them in Palmyra. Then one day their boat sailed into Honolulu harbor with Walker & Stearns. Walker was an ex-convict running from the law, there had been some question if his boat *The Iola* could even make it back to Hawaii. Grahams Yacht was in pristine condition, it was repainted a different color and the name was changed. But a sharp observer, knowledgeable about yachts, was sure it was Graham's yacht. Others went to Palmyra and found more skeletal remains in the water also identified as Muff Graham, his body was never found. Buck Walker was tried and convicted of Graham's murder and was incarcerated in California. He survived his prison term, continued to claim his innocence, they were returning the *Sea Wind* to Hawaii; why Hawaii? Not San Diego, why the color and paint change, why the name change? Stearns was tried separately and found not guilty. The book title "*The Sea Will Tell*," may have more answers. My sympathy goes to the Grahams who lived their dreams only to be murdered by a criminal who should have been behind bars. In antiquity criminals were locked up, now they live among us.

FAMILY-A (580)

The family is the most important unit of society from the very beginning. It was God himself who performed the first wedding in the garden in the beginning of time and ever since then the family has been in trouble. You would think life was perfect and who would have thought of one sibling murdering another sibling in a near perfect world. In my mind a family was my father, my mother, and the seven of us children; that was a family, and I thank God he gave us that model. Now we are told: soon the family will disappear and it certainly begins to look that way. We have psychiatrists, psychologists, marriage counselors, ministers, sex therapists, family clinics, advice columnists, and behavior modification specialists, all of them indicating if you do not get along with your spouse, or children there is someplace to go and give you some wisdom. A counselor and friend once told me that a lot of single people moved here from the mainland, hoping to start a new chapter in their life but forget they brought themselves along, and before long the same issues re-surface. As the Greek poet Ovid (accused of being Greek but really was Italian), said: "Perhaps the grass is greener on the other side because that is where it's watered, how we could miss that? When we were married in New Zealand 64 years ago pastor Deenik preached a sermon about the meaning of Ephesians 5, not very common any more, he explained that what is often counseled here is that Christ was willing to die for his bride the church, but he said the challenge is not to die for the bride but to _live_ for her, that is what seems to be inferred here. We have attended quite a few wedding ceremonies and the ancient custom of a sermon preached at that time seems to have fallen on stony grounds. Now: Let's get married and get on with it, or just move in together and skip the formalities. Every marriage should be a contract between; His, Hers, and Gods. If God is left out the odds of failure are substantially higher. A marriage contract is first submission to God, Husbands and wife submitting to each other, till death do us part, if the love is *a serving love* there is hope. I often think of Christ washing the dirty and dusty feet of his followers, am I prepared to do that? The best illustration we had was seeing dad coming home tired from hard labor and then catering to mom and see to it that her needs were met. Did we think of it on the wedding day? No! We did not, but now on hind site, we understand dad suffered as much as mom did. As a family we witnessed the meaning of *a serving love*. It is our understanding of a family, and are blest to have witnessed that being modeled in a real family. A home that is devoted to serving Christ, may not be the perfect home, but is certainly better then anything else out there.

FAMILY-B (581)

At one of our National Right to Life conventions we invited Dr Harold Voth, a Psychiatrist practicing for 38 years in Kansas City. He was born in 1921 and died in 2015, I got to know him personally at the reception he had much to say; here is some of his speech: _The Castrated Family_. "The crucible from which all life springs is the family. The advance within the family can make or break the individual and collectively civilization. This fundamental Unit is the building block and was the building block of all social organizations: The tribes, The village, & most highly Developed societies and civilizations. Families can survive without the state but without the family all is lost. They make communities which makes a great society. Our nation was built on such people. The Pioneers that started America, possessed great inner strength, they came from strong families, there was no ambiguity about male of female they were given generously by their mothers and fathers. America became the greatest strongest and most generous nation of all time. Industrialization slowly broke up family life. They began to see the fathers less and mothers had to take more responsibilities as a consequence she had less time for homemaking functions. Then came the Wars, One, Two, Korea, & Vietnam. Fathers were killed, million were taken away only to come back a shell of what they once were. Children were denied stable families, and lost their role models they grew up with no fathers. Economic pressures began to build; more & more women were forced into the workplace and more babies were deprived of role models desperately needed during developing years; when a child lacks good parenting he develops various types of disturbances; Young people used to get married now they are living together. Divorce rate is One out of two. The number of unmarried couples is staggering. Children of those incomplete homes, will never develop to their full potential, many will become social liabilities. The impressionable years are the first seven, when the child needs a father and a mother. Millions of children are being reared by single parents and will never have the benefit of growing up in a two parent home. This is why America is coming apart, but that's not all. What is happening to the American male? He is becoming emasculated and women are becoming liberated. If there is a man he is often irresponsible and has no leadership skills. CBS did a series and showed there are 2.2 million so called house husbands. There is a mass exodus of women in the home I had no idea how heavy the women's movement has been infiltrated with lesbians, preschoolers will suffer and society will be destroyed we have thousands of attacks on teachers over hundred murders. Strong Pioneer families created America, only strong families can save it.

TEST TUBE BABIES (582)

At one time medical tradition in our Western civilization rested on the reverence and respect for life holding high the principles set forth by Hippocrates some 2400 years ago. In the preceding 50 years this respect has dwindled to an alarming rate exemplified by the abortion issue along with experimentation on live fetuses in prominent universities in our nation. From a Christian perspective there are some ethical and moral implications here. Therefore let's first establish the fact that scientific knowledge by itself is neither godly nor ungodly and the intense drive of men for exploring the unknown has always been the source of human progress. However by increasing scientific and technological competence we could be in danger of creating a Frankenstein monster that we can not control, the risk is that not all scientists show the same respect when it comes to human life. Here are some points we should ponder, now that Dr Steptoe "*engineered*" the birth of Louise Brown who was conceived in a Petri dish in Britain and subsequent to that experiment she was born on 25 July 1978 according to Newsweek 8/7/'78. The scientists knew the procedure was experimental, but did not tell the patient that no case had ever produced a baby. Louise grew up got married gave birth to a son who was conceived naturally. Here are some issues to ponder: **1**: These experiments are irreversible. **2**: Mrs. Brown would receive the benefit if it failed the baby bore the risk. **3**: The test tube experiment confirmed that life begins at conception. **4**: it separates pro-creation from sexual communion reducing sex to a mere mechanism. **5**: It is divorcing sex from procreation **6**: To allow for a margin of error several eggs are fertilized, what happens to the ones not used **7**: Can it be used to alter genes, making it synonymous with manufacturing. **8**: what is the status of a fertilized egg before re-implantation, are they regarded as humans with rights or are flushed down the drain. **9**: The strong sperm wins the race through the vagina, reducing abnormalities, but in the dish they all have equal chance **10**: Upon perfection can this lead to womb rental, like raising orchids in a nursery? **11**: it does not require the husbands sperm, could this lead to the macho men selling his sperm to the highest bidder. **12**: In a divorce will the husband be required to support a child that is not his, is there legal precedence? God allowed us to participate in the most important aspect of creation; will He be pleased if we take that into our own hands? What about Genesis 2:24 are we saying thanks a lot, we no longer need You and will take it from here. According to Genesis 1:27 we are created in Gods image does that include the test tube? We may be compelled to choose between being out of step with medical technology and being out of step with the Creator of the universe.

INDEPENDENCE DAY (583)

Unrest was growing in the New World and King George III sent troops to control the rebellion. These newcomers wanted to begin a new life and be free from paying taxes to a king no one wanted. In 1776 a committee was formed to initiate a clean break from England, it required some sharp legal minds to produce the needed documents that would set them free from the fatherland. It would be an experiment, there was no model. They found some sharp men who were willing and capable to draft the required papers and begin this task. It was headed by Thomas Jefferson, John Adams, Benjamin Franklin, Philip Livingston, Roger Sherman and others. They called together the Continental Congress in Philadelphia, there was representation of each of the 13 colonies and drafted what became known as the _Declaration of Independence_. Nine voted in favor, Pennsylvania and South Carolina voted NO, New York abstained, meaning the motion was adopted. Twice the following day the Declaration was read to cheering crowds and pealing church bells, proclaiming liberty throughout the land, the bell in the Independence Hall was renamed "_Liberty Bell_". On 4 July 1776 the Declaration of Independence was formally adopted by representatives of the Continental Congress assembled in Philadelphia, signed on behalf of Congress by John Hancock President, and Charles Thomson Secretary. That action officially declared the 13 colonies in the new world a _nation_ they called it The United States. So far so good, but how should this new nation be governed without a king and no Parliament? That was a dilemma, and another conference at Philadelphia drafted the *Articles of Confederation* in 1789 to solve that. Almost immediately following that a group began drafting a Constitution, which was adopted and became the governing document of the United States. These founders understood that times would change and the general thinking of the 1700's my not be the general thinking a few centuries later, therefore 2/3rd of both houses of each state legislature could propose a change and 3/4th of all the states vote in the affirmative, such amendment shall become a part of the governing document of the United States Constitution. James Madison drafted 17 Amendments that were reduced to 12 and past as the first 10 amendments introduced together, and called "*The Bill of Rights*" In summary this is what we are celebrating on Independence-day to be a nation governed by our own adopted rules, instead of a king who inherits his kingdom, we elect a president by majority vote who can only govern for a limited time. Changes must be approved by a legislative body that may be challenged by the Supreme Court as the arbiter if the Constitution they have the final say if any new law or rule is in harmony with the Constitution.

ASCENSION DAY (584)

The observance of this event seems to have been relegated to antiquity, which was the regrettable opinion of Bishop Eusebius, (an Arian Priest who Baptized Constantine the Great on his death bed in the year 337), that was several centuries ago. When I was a young boy in Europe our family worshipped at the Reformed Church and Ascension Day was a serious Holiday, all businesses were closed, and to Christian and none-Christian it was a holiday. The Ascension Day is described in Luke 24:51 and Acts 1:9 it was traditionally celebrated on a Thursday the fortieth day after Easter, although some Christian denominations have moved the observance to the following Sunday calling *that* Ascension Sunday, historically there is a ten day period between Ascension Day (Thursday) and the day of Pentecost Sunday. Several denominations have dropped both of these Christian holidays altogether and only kept Christmas and Easter. Holy Thursday is another name for Ascension Day. In Roman Catholicism the Ascension of the Lord is ranked as a Solemnity and is a Holy Day of Obligation. In the book of common prayer of the Anglican Communion, Holy Thursday is listed as another name for Ascension Day and is a Principal Feast. It seems that in Western Christianity the Feast of Ascension has fallen on hard times. Catholics, Anglicans, some Methodist churches and Eastern Orthodox churches are still holding on to celebrating the Ascension of Jesus in to Heaven as a Holy occasion in Christian History. Christ made us a very serious promise: I will go and prepare a place there for you I will come back and take you to be with me. Thomas said we don't know where you are going so how can we know the way. Jesus said: I am the way and the truth and the life. No one comes to the Father except through me. If you really know me you will know my Father as well. Philip said show us the Father. Jesus said anyone who has seen me has seen the Father. Historically Ascension Day has been an important Holiday but our whole society has taken a major shift to the left, such issues have been moved to less important things. Bishop Eusebius must have had some God given insight into the future because when it concerns issues such as Ascension of our Lord there seems to be less and less interest as we move further into the future. When Jesus predicted that he was leaving and would return to his disciples, there was great interest and that was still so in the 5th century according to the writings of Augustine of Hippo. Some historians believe that prior to the 5th century the Ascension event was often commemorated with the feast of Pentecost. When we were young in Europe during the 1930's and 1940's it was a special holiday for all Christians and non Christians and all were afforded a national holiday, that may be no longer so.

MORAL MAJORITY (585)

In the 1970's a groundswell of conservative Christians rose up in America and Canada who were concerned about the moral decline of North American society aiming to introduce a new social agenda, establishing a strong foundation called _The Moral Majority_. At that time there was a significant connection to the presidential election campaign of Ronald Reagan, who was the lead candidate to be president of America. The person who introduced America to the movement was respected Baptist minister and televangelist Jerry Falwell of Thomas Road Baptist church in Lynchburg Virginia. He was ringing the alarm bells during his half hour daily radio broadcast aired on about 250 stations and a weekly television program that could be seen on 330 Television stations, while he was preaching against abortion, gay rights, Marijuana, and other conservative issues, that were dominating the airwaves at that time. Falwell founded the Moral Majority in 1979, which had a significant influence on the presidential election. The _MM_ also advocated conservative positions on a variety of issues such as Abortion, Gay Rights, Balancing the Budget, Defense Spending, and many more. Its mission was reform America's politics. By the early 1980's it had a membership that was upwards of 2 million and by the mid 1980's it was about twice that. The organization was established with support of various religious and political groups wanting to guide America back to its moorings. The country was recovering from Watergate, and was still reverberating from the political scandals of Watergate which had resulted in the resignation of President Richard Nixon, and most of his advisors either indicted or were already serving time; one of the Presidents key advisors Charles Colson pled guilty and was sent to prison by Judge Sirica. That was not all, on 22 January, 1973 the United States Supreme Court ruled that unborn children were not entitled to live, our constitution allowed for abortion up to the point of birth, even though the constitution was silent on that issue, the left wanted it. Yes America was adrift and the church of the 20th century was by necessity forced to deal with issues it had never seen before and was ill prepared to deal with it. America was pulled further and further away from its foundation, and the *MM* attempted to work with Grassroots groups but the momentum was moving in the opposite direction. As expected the *MM* faced severe criticism from political liberals and moderates, who accused them of pushing religion on a secular society. Pat Robertson was an ally of Falwell and led the TV program called *the 700 club*, which became the flagship of Christian broadcasting. Pat Robertson and I did a joint Pro-Life seminar in Denver. He was an icon, and died at age 93 on 8 June 2023.

WATERGATE SCANDAL (586)

The Watergate Complex is a group of six buildings, offices, and apartments; and is one of the most desirable living places in Washington DC, popular with members of Congress. It's a group of buildings covering 10 acres of land in the Capital. It housed the headquarters of the Democratic National Committee located on the sixth floor of the office building. Someone had broken in the DNC office, wiretapped phones, and photographed documents, which became the _Scandal of the Century_ resulting eventually in resignation of President Richard Nixon. The crime was referred to as the Watergate Scandal and revealed some egregious presidential actions which eventually prompted the House Judiciary Committee to approve three articles of impeachment against the President. As the hearings and investigations moved forward it became inevitable that President Richard Nixon was going to be the second President in American history to be impeached, (_Andrew Johnson in 1868 was the first_). When Nixon's public, and political, support had completely eroded, he was beginning to see the _"handwriting on the wall"_, we saw it too, and on 9 August, 1974 President Richard Nixon resigned from office, the only president in over 200 year of American history that has done so. One month later on 8 September 1974, his successor, President Gerald Ford, pardoned him. In total 69 people were indicted and 48 of them were officials in the Nixon Administration. During that time Evangelical leaders were meeting in Washington and praying for the country; I was at several of those meetings, and we took turns to emcee the breakfast meetings where notable speakers were invited. When it was my turn, to emcee, Chuck Colson was the speaker and at that time he had not yet appeared before the Judge. Colson had only just become a new Christian the month before and told us; all these officials would be pleading innocent, but Colson stated I know I am guilty therefore pray for me, I will be pleading guilty before the no nonsense Federal Judge John Sirica. I know what I have done and will not stand before a holy God and say I am innocent, when I am not. He did indeed plead guilty, and was the first person of the Watergate Scandal to be sent to prison. Colson served his time and after his release became one of the most powerful ambassadors of the King of Kings, he founded Prison Fellowship, a ministry that has now spread throughout the world, and wrote more then 30 books; God used him till the day he died at age 80 on 21 April 2012, and even more so after, through his writings. All the other presidential advisors were tried and convicted. It became clear that Washington had *"cleaned the swamp"*. Well, not quite! Corruption is like an infection unless the poison is removed it returns, and it already has with greater vengeance.

PENTECOST (587)

Pentecost is a Christian holiday; it is the seventh Sunday, or 50th day, after Easter, and commemorates the descent of the Holy Spirit upon the Apostles and other followers of Jesus who were in Jerusalem, as recorded in Acts 2. At one time here in America it was an event of great significance, but lately it seems to have taken a back seat on the list of Christian holidays. In some circles it is known as the "_Feast of Weeks_" and in the rabbinic tradition the "_Feast of 50 days_." Ireland also calls it Whitsunday, (_meaning; wearing white robes_). Acts 2 refers to a sound like the blowing of a violent wind from heaven that filled the whole house and tongues of fire came to rest on each of them all were filled and began to speak in other tongues; the foreign people that were present, were hearing some gibberish? No! They heard their own language. Pentecostalism, in the Charismatic religious movement gave rise to a number of churches in the US to be unique in its belief that all should seek a post conversion experience called "_baptism with the Holy Spirit_" believing that 20th century Christians require an experience of speaking in tongues. In my capacity of being the executive director of Evangelical Churches I was asked a few times: "Terry do you have the gift?" I asked what you mean. Both answers were the same, are you born again and have the gift, if not, u are not born again. I thought I was born again but the only "_tongues_" I can speak, are the three languages I grew up with in Europe, and the two additional ones I learned after. One pastor offered to teach me how to speak in tongues. I declined, and told him if God gives me the gift I will not resist it. If I understand the Scripture correctly; it is a gift of God, and if He gives me that gift I will rejoice and will not resist it. We left it that way, because I liked him as a friend. I have spoken in most churches here in the Islands either as a representative of the Gideon's or replaced a pastor while he traveled, or gave a political report from one of my trips to Washington DC. I have discovered that the practice varies greatly. Some set a time aside where the entire church speaks in tongues at the same time, even shouting at the top of their voice while some stand on their seat. Others do it in private at home. In all cases I have never heard an interpreter. In relation to that, have been offered Hermann Zaiss, Aimee McPherson, Oral Roberts, Kathryn Kuhlman and Benny Hinn but prefer the Word of God. Sometime ago we had meetings in the Anatole Hotel in Dallas and on Sunday took a Cab to visit Oak Cliff Bible, (a black church) where we had wanting to go for some time to listen to Dr Tony Evans who said this: "The Holy Spirit brings the words of the Bible into your heart, then puts his seal on it, and only God can break the seal; Dr Evans then asked: If you believe u are a Christian, is there enough evidence to convict you?"

CRUSADES (588)

Let's first define the Crusades. They are a series of religious wars, and/or military expeditions, to the Holy Land between 1095 and 1291 intended to recapture Jerusalem and its surroundings from Islamic rule. With the first crusade in about 1095, Pope Urban II proclaimed the first expedition at the Council of Clermont which was a mixed Synod of Ecclesiastics and Layman. The pope encouraged military support for Byzantine emperor Alexios I Komnenos and called for an armed pilgrimage to Jerusalem. In Western Europe there was enthusiastic support and participants came from the entire continent. Initially there were four crusader states: <u>County of Edessa</u>, <u>Principality of Antioch</u>, <u>County of Tripoli</u>, and the <u>Kingdom of Jerusalem</u>. A European presence remained in the region till the fall of Acre in 1291 after that enthusiasm had dwindled down to no interest. Not too many were organized after that it ended except for some against Christians, but most were less religious in nature, and a little more political such as the struggle of Christians against the Ottoman Empire was a conflict between Christians and Muslims in the Iberian Peninsula it was proclaimed a crusade in 1123 and ended in 1492 with the fall of Emirate of Granada. From 1147 campaigns in Northern Europe against pagan tribes were considered crusades. In 1199, Pope Innocent III began the practice of declaring them crusades against what the Latin Church considered *heretic* Christian communities. Crusades were called against the Cathars in Languedoe and against Bosnia;

against the Waldensians in Savoy and the Hussites in Bohemia, (*Jan Hus, a serious Bible teacher, was burned at the stake by the established church in Prague in 1415*), and in response to the rise of the Ottoman Empire. There were also some popular Crusades that were unsanctioned by the church. The term crusades have been applied to conflicts in the 11th, 12th, and 13th century, and there has been great diversity in understanding the Crusades which is still a matter of debate. The meaning of these crusades are generally viewed as *Traditionalists* only those of the Holy Land, *Pluralists* see it as Military expeditions with papal endorsements, *Popularists*, focus on the groundswells of religious fervor, and *Generalists* see it as the basic phenomenon of Latin Holy Wars. Some historians consider it a combination of two or three of these, in the beginning the word pilgrimage might have been a better fit, although there was strong animosity between the established church and what we might call Evangelicalism evidenced by the fact that followers of Hus (called Hussites), who years later were relentlessly persecuted by the church. In 1415 the crusades had ended, were they successful? That depends on the definition of success. The church was powerful and the clergy loved control.

TITANIC (589)

The RMS Titanic was a British passenger liner, its length was 889 ft (270 m) which sank in the North Atlantic Ocean on 15 April, 1912 after striking an iceberg during its maiden voyage from Southampton to New York it was the largest ship afloat at the time. On board were 2453 passengers & crew and about 1500 died, making it the deadliest sinking of a single ship at that time. The passenger facilities were at the highest standard of luxury. There were First, Second, and Third class cabins, and a 7 ft deep saltwater swimming pool, gymnasium, Turkish bath, Steam Room, and a Massage room all lavishly decorated, a Lounge in the style of the Palace of Versailles, an enormous reception room, a men's smoking room and a reading and writing room. There was an *a la carte* restaurant in the style of the Ritz Hotel designed by a famous Italian restaurateur. A café decorated in the style of a French sidewalk café. Passengers could enjoy the finest French cuisine in the most luxurious of surroundings. There was a Veranda Café where light refreshments were offered. Although it was primarily a passenger ship it carried a substantial amount of cargo; there was a post office on board that carried mail under contract with the Royal Mail and was manned by 5 postal clerks handling 60,000 letters and mail items, the ship carried 19,455 cubic feet of first and second class baggage. It exhibited a painting valued at $100,000 ($2.1 million in today's value), only lifeboats for half the people. The sheer size of the vessel had posed an engineering challenge; and before it was launched on its maiden voyage the ship made two sea trials consisting of a number of tests in open ocean waters traveling about 570 nautical miles distance, and was declared sea-worthy. It was launched for its maiden voyage with a crew of about 885 people of which 97% were male and 23 were stewardesses. Captain Edward John Smith had served 40 years at sea therefore was considered highly qualified to command a vessel this size, but since the Titanic was new, it was a first for all. (*Having made 17 ocean trips by ship, the first days u explore the ship*), and the Titanic was no different. The beginning passed without incident, although the crew was aware of ice in the vicinity, they did not reduce the speed and continued to steam at 22 knots (25 mph), (*that speed was later criticized as reckless by experienced sailors*), in spite of the fact that this ship was unsinkable, they considered timekeeping more important than caution. The ship had just collided with an iceberg and sunk within 2 hour, 40 Min, other ships had too they always completed their journey and this one was unsinkable. There were only life-boats for half the people. The Captain is believed to have gone down with the ship. It was the calamity of the century.

TIANANMEN SQUARE PROTEST 1989 (590)

In 1989 we were visiting China and our guide Crystal told us there was a major unrest brewing among the students and she was going to be a lead person at the student-led protest the following day at Tiananmen Square. It was scheduled by the students who had been disadvantaged by the govt. The protests were precipitated by the death of pro-reform Chinese Communist Party (CCP) leader _Hu Yaobang_ in April 1989 amid rapid economic development and social change in post-Mao China. Like all changes, it benefited some, and disadvantaged others. Crystal was a friend so we took the side of the students and I told her I will march with u, as far as we understood, all these students wanted was Liberty which became even more clear when we saw them carry a replica of the Statue of Liberty then we really knew we were on the right side. But Crystal persuaded us to escape to Hong Kong; she said I do not know what will be done to Americans. It did not look any better when the tanks rolled into the Square and it became obvious this was not America. There the tanks would have stopped for the bikes and the demonstrators, but this was China, here in the squire the tanks mowed right over them. We saw the handwriting on the wall, specially when that kind Crystal insisted that we escape while we could, she dropped us at the airport, we exchanged addresses and promised to write; we boarded the HK flight and from there to

Honolulu. At home we watched the World Press the news was not pretty. The following month I wrote Crystal a letter sent her some promised tapes but got no response. After two attempts we asked our friends who ministered at Peking Medical School where Crystal was a student. They tried to locate her but she was never found. According to International media reports thousands of students died, China will not release those figures. I went back to China two more times, was expected to be refused entry due to my internet commentaries aired about the massacre at the Squire. The commentaries were refused but they never connected me to the one hour Hymn program, as far as I can tell _it_ may still be running there. The students wanted reform; since Covit we have not been back; am not sure if my commentaries are still running in China? My Guangdong contact is not sure. The 1978 reformist leaders had hoped that policies under Deng Xiaoping would get better especially with regards to the job market for students. After Deng's 18 August 1980 speech titled "_Reform_"; like most other China rhetoric that's all it was. When nothing came of that on 21 April 1981, 100,000 students marched on Tiananmen Square. We keep praying for the Chinese students, but don't think any reform will happen soon; we are concerned about Hong Kong. We love the China people who extended the olive branch to us, (not their leaders; they only want power.)

BUBONIC PLAGUE (591)

The Bubonic plague raged through Europe and North Africa about the same time the crusaders came to a close and it was generally assumed that they had carried the disease in to Europe. According to a brilliant historian that taught us about 70 years ago in Europe, he was convinced that such thinking has no basis in fact and may have been just speculation by some who were strong opponents of the crusades. He made point that no one really seems to know where the plague originated, even though some think it was the crusades, other say it may have been Chinese merchant ships, but all is pure speculation. It has been commonly referred to as *The Bubonic plague* but some have coined it *The Black Death*. What is not speculative is that it *is* highly contagious and came mostly from fleas that were carried by infected rodents, and in the 14th century it swept through China, India, Persia, Russia, Italy, France, England, Germany, and pretty much through the world. More then 10 million people died from the horrible disease, just in the city of London 150,000 people died from the plague, in Europe it killed about a third of the total population. It was a long time ago, but what we do know is that it spread virtually through the entire world. And we know that it was a serious epidemic at a time when medical knowledge about it was somewhat limited and still developing. It may be why so many people were contracting the disease. Treatment was limited in the 14th century, which may be one of the reasons the death toll was so high. Infection can be the result of a flea bite, handling dead animals, disposing of rodents, or being careless about treatment. Without treatment the chances are 30–90% will result in death. People who have been affected need antibiotic within 24 hours, there are now vaccines available and it is wise to seek medical attention if bit by a flea. Globally between 2010 and 2015, (_that is recent_) there were 3248 confirmed cases, which resulted in 584 deaths. For the time the disease was raging throughout the world in the 14th century the then known statistical date indicates there were 10 million deaths but WHO believe it may have been as high as 50 million. The disease is carried by field rats or those we find in our homes, and more is known about it now, and it is important to seek immediate medical advice. In the 1300's not much was known about the plague, meaning there was also not much known about prevention. Antibiotic is a must and medical attention is important. The Democratic Republic of the Congo had 1000 to 2000 cases last year according to the World Health Organization, meaning the disease is still with us.

KRISTALLNACHT (592)

Many of my readers already know that I grew up as a child in Europe under Hitler, using my multi linguistic abilities here, Kristallnacht means: _Night of broken glass_. Hitler mostly hid in his bunker, therefore are we blaming him here for something he did <u>not</u> do? All of Europe particularly those who worked in Dachhau, Auschwitz and the other 1000 camps, witnessed, or participated, in the atrocities; God gave each of us a mind to discern right from wrong. I was a little boy under age 10; even we did what we could, such as stretching a wire across the road so that soldiers would trip and fall or tried to derail the train, put rocks on the tracks; childish? Well, <u>we were children</u> but we tried. Perhaps Kristallnacht is why I feel so strong that all of Europe is responsible. Our parents did what they could and were willing to take risk by accepting Jewish children and hide them from the soldiers and the traitors. But the masses did nothing being afraid _"they might get hurt"_ and we know <u>you would get hurt</u> if you did stand up against the Wearmacht. It might be your life. Why did it have to be a young 21 year old girl who stood up against the Nazi's and when she discovered the cost might be her life, <u>she did not back down,</u> even when offered an out, she stood up for what is right. If more had been willing to say: _Enough is enough,_ like this young German girl <u>Sophie Scholl,</u> who knew right from wrong and was willing to say so. How is it that this 21 year old girl was willing to say _No More_! All excuses at the Nuremburg trial did not come from Nazi leaders, but came from

Nazi cowards: "*Hitler made me do it*" It's the same excuse we used when we were about 6 or 7 and told dad about our sister: *she made me do it*, hoping she would get the punishment. We learned it from these generals at Nuremburg. Here is a prime example: *the destruction of Kristallnacht* on that night Jewish homes, hospitals, and schools, were ransacked; buildings were demolished with sledgehammers; 267 synagogues were destroyed throughout Germany, Austria, and other European countries. Over 7,000 Jewish businesses were damaged or destroyed and 30,000 Jewish men were arrested and incarcerated in concentration camps many of them never came back. 91 were murdered, estimates of total fatalities are not known. Some historians put the figures a lot higher; it was open season on Jews. Kristallnacht was a prelude to the final solution during the Holocaust. My own father is no longer with us, but it still hurts when a young soldier with a gun shouted to my dad who was (*25 yrs his senior*), *do as I say*! What scares me is this: Germans are, and looked like us, therefore I ask the same question Wiesenthal asked in his book the Sunflower: "*What would u have done?*" Could it happen again? If you are an extreme leftist and drink the cool aid you likely see nothing, hear nothing and know nothing.

PETRA (593)

Petra is an historical and archaeological city located in the Arabic country of Jordan it is believed to have been inhabited from as early as 7000 BC and the Nabataeans might have settled in what would become the capital city of their kingdom as early as the 4th century BC. It is a fascinating city. Sometime ago we had meetings in Amman and decided to take a break from our meetings and hike in there. It was hot and I walked in with Rob and Becky. Rob was a retired fighter pilot, him and Becky had some interest to hike in there as well, although Becky was not well she was a real trooper and said, if we make it all the way in, Terry will you ride a camel back with me we did that and rented 2 camels going back; it was my first camel ride, but prefer my Honda over that camel, it made a serious attempt to eat my shoe. The trading business gained the Nabataeans considerable revenue, Petra became the focus of their wealth, and unlike their enemies they were accustomed to living in the barren deserts, were able to repel attacks by taking advantage of the area's mountainous terrain. They were particularly skillful in harvesting rainwater. Petra flourished in the 1st century AD. Then their importance declined after an earthquake in 363 which destroyed many structures. It remained largely unknown to the western world until 1812 when Swiss travelers rediscovered it. Famous for its rock-cut architecture it has often been called the Rose City because of the color of the stone from which it is carved. It has been a UNESCO World Heritage Site since 1985. In 2007 Petra was voted one of the 7 Wonders of the World, and I can see why, I am glad we made time to take a day off and hike in there. In 2019 it claimed to have been visited by 1.1 million tourists per year. On the way in we were pointed out that the mountain on our left was the location of the tomb of Aaron. At the end of the narrow gorge you see Al-Khazneh, (known as) the Treasury hewn into the sandstone cliff, remaining in remarkably preserved condition, a little further is en-Nejr a massive Theatre that was cut into the hillside and into several of the tombs. The theatre was said to hold 8.500 people; audiences were entertained with Poetry-Reading, Gladiator-Fights, and Drama. The Petra Pool and Garden complex is a series of structures that took significant damage in the 363 Galilee earthquakes. The high place of sacrifice is located at the top of Jebel Mountain which is an 800 step hike, but Becky was not up to it so we did not go there. It is commonly believed that animal sacrifices took place on that mountain nevertheless it is a sacred site for Muslims. In honor of this, a goat was sacrificed there annually other rituals also took place such as the burning of frankincense. We had landed deep in Biblical history, back in Amman there was the wall where Uriah died; it was a memorable visit.

GREAT AWAKENING (594)

Most historians consider Anglican minister Jonathan Edwards and British minister George Whitefield to be the chief fathers of the *Great Awakening* of the 1700's. They worked closely with the Wesley Brothers who made several trips to the Colonies, even though they differed on Armenianism which was embraced by the Wesley's. That originated when Professor Jacobus Arminius, of the Leiden University debated Franciscus Gomarus who was a Calvinist. They differed on election, which the Synod of Dort (1618) dealt with. Wesley's agreed with Arminius; Edwards took the side of Gomarus who preached Calvinism, they agreed to disagree. (Armenianism also had a more liberal version which embraced Universalism). The 1700's is also referred to as the age of reason. It was a plus for renewed interest in the sciences; Whitefield often traveled from town to town, which resulted in renewed dedication toward religion. Historians believe that such powerful preaching had a lasting impact on the culture in the colonies in more ways then one, meaning the Great Awakening moved the country forward at a faster pace. Edwards and Whitefield made lasting inroads in the Colonies their teaching also had other effects on development of the America we came to know in the 1950's. The colonies were quasi religiously divided; most of New England became Congregational, Middle America became Anglican, Lutheran, Baptist, Presbyterians and Dutch Reformed, and the Southern Colonies were more Baptists, Presbyterians and Quakers; in the 1720's there was a renewed emphasis on Calvinism, brought in by Edwards who was passionate about conversion which he documented in his book "_Narratives of Surprising Conversions_". Whitefield placed more emphasis on preaching and teaching while he traveled 5000 miles, preaching 350 times a year, his style was charismatic, theatrical, and expressive. Edwards' religion was more formal which led to a great recommitment to church attendance, overall result was renewed dedication to Christianity _he_ preached mostly in his home parish. The Pioneers of the new world had great industrial success while the Great awakening filled in the spiritual dimensions. Whitefield preached more then 18000 sermons and could speak to audiences up to 30,000 people his voice was like a trumpet. Edwards died of a vaccination shot against smallpox; he and Sarah had 11 children leaving a legacy of descendents that included 30 judges, 100 lawyers, 13 college presidents, 100 professors, 75 military officers, 3 senators, 3 mayors, 3 governors and 1 vice president, 80 got elected to public office, he is credited with the most powerful sermon titled: "_Sinners in the hands of an angry God_" available on CD presented by Max Mc Clean, heard it twice, powerful!

NORTH KOREA (595)

For nearly 1500 years Korea was a unified country until it was divided into North and South after World War II, (similar to *the division of East & West Germany, although they re-united 45 yrs later*); Korea's line is referred to as demilitarized zone, and was armed with an electrified barrier between the two Korea's who are now hopelessly separated by cultural ideologies, and with the Sino-Soviet split in 1960, the North Korean leader Kim disliked Khrushchev so he turned to the Chinese; but relationship with China where an aging Mao was loosing his grip on power, was complicated at best. To make matters worse, in 1967 Mao initiated the Cultural Revolution which Kim denounced, although he began his own idea of self reliance and more independence for North Korea, but experienced frequent and severe famines; one of them, in the 1990's resulted in the death of about 400,000 people. In 1994 the 84 year old Kim died of a heart attack and his son Kim Yung IL succeeded him, as the Supreme leader of North Korea. Kim Jung Un is his son and only 2nd in line to assume leadership, but a when Kim Jung Il died his successor Kim Jong-nam had been assassinated in Malaysia leaving Kim Jong Un to be the next leader of North Korea. (*North Korea is a closed country we may never discover what goes on behind the scene in the power struggles among family members, specially when the stakes are high*); all we have is speculation about who really is the controlling person there; is it the little fat boy *Kim Jung Un*, or is it his younger sister *Kim Yo-Jung*? There are reports that Kim had his girlfriend executed for violating pornography laws; another report states that his uncle Jang Song-thaek was arrested and executed by firing squad for treachery. Multiple reports point to extensive executions within the family even children and grand children. In January 2013, the UN High Commissioner for human rights pointed too multiple human rights violations in North Korea, suggesting that Kim could, and should, be held accountable for crimes against humanity; some have referred to him as madman, after the death of his half brother _Kim Jong-nam_. He has proudly claimed that the country had great success in combating the COVID-10 pandemic and had no confirmed cases, although medical experts doubt his claim. Apparently all of the Kim family children have studied in Europe in a private International School at Berne in Gumligen Switzerland which indicates they have experienced some degree of freedom, or at least have tasted liberty, which is absent in North Korea; Kim Yo-Jung is reported to be the devil in person; is there hope for the people of North Korea? First Christian missionary Robert Thomas from Wales was killed there in 1866, it's not much better today, as long as the little fat man with his sister rules.

MASADA (596)

Masada is an ancient fortification in the Southern district of Israel; we had a choice whether we should go there or go on our way to Egypt, in the end we decided to fly to Cairo and let Masada go. There are enough areas of interest in the region we could have stayed a year, but were also quite happy to see Cairo in the limited time we had. Masada was one of two palaces built by _Herod the Great_ on top of a mountain, located on the eastern edge of the Judean Desert overlooking the Dead Sea east of Arad. Herod's palaces were built for himself, not so much to have a place with a nice view but more so to feel safe from his enemies such as the Romans. We were advised that Masada is one of Israel's most popular tourist attractions and it has become a toss up between Jerusalem and Masada. According to Josephus the siege by Roman troops from 73 to 74 at the end of the First Jewish–Roman War ended in mass suicide of the 960 Sicarii rebels who were hiding there. There is some ambiguity about the facts but this is what we learned. At the top on the plateau to the east it abruptly ends at a cliff steeply falling straight down about 400 m (1300 ft), in the other direction to the west, the cliff is about 80 m (300 ft). The top of the mesa-like plateau is flat, 550 m (1800 ft) x 270 m (890 ft). Around the plateau Herod had built a 4 m (13 ft high) casemate wall around the entire plateau. On that level area he built a fortress which contained storehouses, barracks, an armory, a palace and a series of cisterns (capacity around 40,000 cubic meters) that were refilled with rainwater, a single day's rain allegedly could support 1,000 people for 2 to 3 years. Josephus writes that in the first-Century the site was fortified by Hasmonean ruler Alexander Janna us. It is believed that about 37 to 31 BCE Herod built the large fortress on the plateau as a refuge mostly for himself and in the event of a revolt he had two palaces built stocked with an endless food supply. According to Josephus the Sicarii rebel group overcame the Roman garrison in about 66 CE, or AD. He might have based his narration upon commentaries of the Roman commanders that he had contact with. Roman governor of Judea, Lucius Flavius Silva laid siege to Masada in 73 CE and breached the wall of the fortress with a battering ram then crushed the Jewish resistance at Masada. When they broke through the soldiers discovered all food storerooms ablaze and about 960 men, women and children had either killed each other or committed suicide, only 28 bodies were found. Two women and five children were found alive. Masada was last occupied during the Byzantine period (*often referred to as the continuing period after the Roman Empire*); they established a small church at the site.

ARTICLES OF CONFEDERATION (597)

The Articles of Confederation was an agreement among the 13 states of the United States, (*formerly referred to as the thirteen Colonies*), served as the nation's first frame of government. It was debated by the Second Continental Congress at Independence Hall in Philadelphia between July 1776 and November 1777 and finalized on November 15, 1777. It was then ratified by all 13 colonial states. A guiding principle of the articles was the establishment and preservation of the independence and sovereignty of the states providing clearly written rules for how the states' league of friendship, known as the Perpetual Union would be organized. Soon more states became convinced that a meeting was needed to revise the Articles and indeed a meeting was called in Philadelphia in May 1787; *that* became the Constitutional Convention and the delegates soon realized it was not possible to revise the articles and there was a need to replace it with a new constitution. That was done; the New Constitution provided for a much stronger federal government by establishing a chief executive, (*the president*), *courts*, and *taxing powers*. Benjamin Franklin proposed the Albany Plan, an inter-colonial collaboration to help solve mutual local problems. Over the next several decades some of the problems were addressed and strengthen the new nation. In 1775 the second Continental Congress began acting as the provincial government for the

United Colonies. Most states felt the new nation must have a written constitution, a rulebook for how the new nation should function. During the war, Congress exercised an unprecedented level of political, diplomatic, military, issues fiat money, negotiated with foreign governments, and economic authority. It adopted trade restrictions, established and maintained an army. The records of the second Congress show the need for a declaration of independence. In June 1776 Richard Henry Lee introduced a resolution to declare independence. A committee was appointed to draft such a document; John Dickinson Pennsylvania chaired that committee of 13. The committee met frequently, their final results were presented to the Congress, after approval the articles of Confederation were sent to the Colonies for ratification. All, (except Maryland), ratified but after two years they too came on board, meaning it was agreed to by all the Colonies now changed to the United States. Congress was informed of Maryland's assent on March 1, 1781, and officially proclaimed the Articles of Confederation to be the law of the land. On March 4 1789 The rules were superseded by the United States Constitution as authored by the Continental Congress.

BLACK PANTHER PARTY (598)

The Black Panther Party was a Marxist-Leninist, Black Power Political Organization founded in the US by college students _Bobby Seale_ and _Huey P. Newton_ in Oct 1966 in Oakland California. After World War II tens of thousands of black people left the southern states, and moved to Oakland and other cities in the Bay area to find work in such industries as Kaiser Shipyards; it was the _Second Great Migration_. Sweeping changes altered the once white-dominated demographics; blacks concentrated in poor urban ghettos with high unemployment, substandard housing, and were mostly excluded from political representation, top universities, and the middle class. Police departments were all white; only 16 of Oakland's 661 police force were black. Civil Rights tactics proved incapable of redressing these conditions. In May 1967, the Panthers (in a publicity stunt) invaded the State Assembly Chamber in Sacramento with guns in hand and scared a lot of people. At that time they had almost no following. That year the Mulford Act was past which repealed the law allowing the public carrying of loaded firearms without a permit; it was named after California Assemblyman Don Mulford, and was signed into law by Governor Ronald Reagan. Its goal was disarming members of the Black Panther Party who were conducting armed patrols in Oakland neighborhoods. Awareness of the Black Panther Party grew rapidly; it was active in the US between 1966 and 1982 with chapters in San Francisco, Los Angeles, New York, Chicago and most major US cities. In 1967 they published their 10 point

"_What we want program_" **1**. Freedom, **2** full employment of our people, **3**. End of robbery by Capitalists, **4**. Decent housing, fit for shelter of human beings, **5** Education that teaches true history and our role in present society, **6**. Black man to be exempt from military service, **7**. End police brutality and murder of black people, **8**. Freedom for all black man in federal state and county prisons and jails, **9**. All court trials to have jury of their peers representing the black community, **10** we want land, bread, housing, education, clothing, and justice. The Panthers were active in many prisons and had an international chapter in the UK and Algeria. The party advocated for class struggle claiming to represent the proletarian vanguard. In 1969, J. Edgar Hoover (director FBI) described the party as the greatest threat to America's internal security. The FBI infiltrated the party with an illegal and covert counterintelligence program of surveillance, infiltration, perjury, police harassment, all designed to undermine their criminal activity. The Black Panther Party members were involved in many fatal firefights with police. After 1982 the party suffered a number of internal conflicts and lost momentum, membership declined, it's a very different party today.

AFFIRMATIVE ACTION (599)

The US Supreme court decided June 2003 in a 6–3 decision that race conscious admission policies of the University of North Carolina and Harvard College violate the Constitution, effectively ending affirmative action, of the Bakke case, in higher education and for that matter in any business that has employees. It is beyond question that this ruling will reverberate across campuses nationwide, although the rulings fell along ideological lines; Chief Justice John Roberts wrote the majority opinion Gorsuch, Kavanaugh, and Justice Thomas, (*who has never been silent about the issue*), wrote concurring opinions, Alito and Amy Coney Barrett concurred. Justice Sotomayor and Kagan dissented; (it is here where I paused, I am not a lawyer, and this may be above my pay-grade, but wanted to guess Justice Ketanji Jackson's opinion, because I had watched her confirmation hearing and predicted accurately what she would say.) Although on this particular case she had conflict of interest and rightfully recused herself, she could not resist expressing herself, which turned out to be almost exactly what I had assumed she would do, I could virtually give you that on every opinion of her from here on. She is an open book radical that is why she was confirmed by the left; it is not what the founders had in mind; a justice was supposed to be, she could not even be on the list. But we are a few centuries past the founders so why listen to them. The 1978 Bakke decision was flawed and we knew it could never stand, just like Dred Scott of 1857, (although the court did not reversed it, the congress did).

It is what is called checks & balances. With regards to this case Sotomayor & Kegan are left; their rulings are expected and in some cases may even go both sides that are not so with Jackson, she is on a mission and should have never been confirmed. Is she the unfixable hairline crack in the glass? Roberts wrote: "*race based*" admission guidelines cannot be reconciled with the guarantees of the Equal Protection Clause, the first circuit found that Harvard's consideration of race has resulted in fewer admissions of Asian-American students, respondents assertion that race is never a negative factor in their admissions program cannot withstand scrutiny; college admissions are a benefit to some applicants but not to others necessarily advantages the former at the expense of the latter. Colleges and universities will no longer be allowed to seek greater diversity of their student bodies by preferencing race, although student applicants will not be precluded from discussing their race during the application process as it relates to their individual experience. The most immediate effect will be a decrease in the number of Black and Latino students admitted to the most selective schools.

UFO'S (600)

A UFO is an (_Unidentified Flying Object_), and an UAP is an _Unidentified Aerial Phenomena;_ the million dollar question: Is it a hoax, or is it real? I can answer that, here it is: "_I don't know!_" Perhaps aliens live among us, and are back in vogue in a big way; their popularity is approaching levels we have not seen for some time, and if it's that popular it must be real. Recently former US Navy fighter pilot Alex Dietrich spoke on 60 Minutes about a strange encounter with a UFO she had in November 2004. As a Ltd Cmdr she logged 1250 flying hours 375 of the carrier; has an MBA, and a degree in Civil Engineering, and said she was training 100 miles southwest of the coast of San Diego, California and saw an stormy spot in an otherwise calm ocean and up came this aerial vehicle ascending 80,000 ft in less then a second. She said: its now 3 children later and I never think about it; what is left of it is just a blimp. Some dictionaries refer to UFO's as extraterrestrials perhaps that could stand a little updating. Defense agencies across the globe might be facing spy planes from a rival nation. There is a gaping chasm between seeing something in the sky that can not be explained, and believing we might be facing visitors from another planet. We live in an age of airspace incursions, drones, and incomprehensible guests; there is no shortage on investigations and sightings by credible people who have shared what they saw. Although this issue is above my pay grade, but as far as I can tell there is no life in the solar system, despite what some _Mars fanatics_ might have u believe. Having said that, I will quickly agree that there are tough questions about these issues that are real and _not_ come from the lunatic frenzies. Here are some: Where do these spacecraft come from? How do they get here? Why did no one see them arrive? Why are they here and what is their mission? Is it malevolent? Is it demonic? They are breaking the law of physics an experienced pilot says ascending 80,000 ft in less then a second; should we revisit our understanding of the law of physics? Are they human? If not what are they? Are they scientifically far ahead of us? What <u>can</u>, or <u>should</u>, we do? _1_: We humble ourselves ask God to give us wisdom; and clear understanding from our Heavenly Father, it is not required that all people pray, only that some bow seriously before Almighty God and ask him to open our eyes. _2_: Work in collegial style across the world; research science is generally not political, but about accruing evidence with repeated observations, all data should be fed into one central computer system, all who contribute to funding share in discovery. America's leading Universities could submit a global request to all Universities and begin with existing current data. Such has been done before; discovery is open to all.

BERMUDA TRIANGLE (601)

The Bermuda Triangle; is it an urban legend, is it a myth, or is it real? In September 1950 the media alerted us to the real danger with headlines such as "_Sea Mystery at our Back door_". Articles reported of planes and ships, including the loss of flight 19 that simply had been swallowed up in thin air or the ocean graveyard. What do you do when major ships and airplanes disappear over a large ocean area and never get found, such as US Navy ships and torpedo bombers on training missions, (according to media reports), just vanished; the article laid out the now familiar triangular area where these losses took place, as well as the supernatural element of the flight-19 incident, the flight leader had been heard saying: We are entering white water, nothing seems right, we don't know where we are, the water is green, no white; the reporter wrote that the plane flew of to Mars. Some 1964 articles were headlined "_The Deadly Bermuda Triangle_" and talked about disappearances that became a pattern of strange events in the region, enough to make you loose sleep, others expanded and catered to those who relished mystery stories, there was no shortage of actual incidences, to make it more sensational some of the titles changed from Bermuda Triangle to _The Devils Triangle_ in the early 1970's. The triangle is about 1,500,000 sq miles, with some stretching east as far as the Irish coast. It was about that time that we got invited to attend business meetings in Bermuda at the Southampton Hotel. When we shared it with some friends, they advised us don't go if you want to come home. We did not heed that counsel and have since had two most enjoyable meetings at the Southampton Hotel in Bermuda. Were not able to get a rental car, due to the limited number of automobiles permitted on the island, so we rented a scooter and were able to see most of the island during our free time, even interviewed the Town Crier, (who brought back memories of the 1940's in Europe when we could only get news from the town crier). Then in 1975 a new article surfaced "*The Bermuda Triangle Mystery Solved*". The number of ships and aircrafts reported missing in the area had not been significantly greater than any other ocean or sky losses according to Lloyds of London. The tropical cyclones were normal for that area, not mysterious. The media had consistently exaggerated the numbers by sloppy research, and some reported losses never happened. The sensationalism of the Bermuda Triangle was *exactly that*, SENSATIOINAL. Fabrications, misconceptions, manufactured stories, do sell newspapers. The fact that planes crash, and ships sink, made us realize that we live in the real world and not in a fairy tale wonderland. The Bermuda Triangle Sensation may well have been the hoax of the century.

MALAYSIA AIRLINES FLIGHT 370 (602)

Malaysia Airlines Flight 370 disappeared on 8 March 2014 while flying from Kuala Lumpur International airport in Malaysia to its planned destination, Beijing International Airport in China. With 227 passengers and 12 crew members. 38 Minutes after take off when the flight was over the South China Sea contact with the Boeing 777-200ER was lost and has till this day never been re-established. It was tracked by the Malaysian military primary radar system for another hour deviating westward from its planned flight path and left radar range northwest of Penang Island in northwestern Peninsular Malaysia. The search for the missing airplane became the most expensive search in the history of aviation. The lack of official information in the days immediately after the disappearance prompted fierce criticism from the Chinese public, particularly from relatives of the passengers, as most people on board were of Chinese origin. Pieces of debris washed ashore in the western Indian Ocean were confirmed to be from Flight 370. After a three-year search by joint agencies across 46,000 sq miles failed to locate the missing aircraft, without success, further search was forced to be suspended; even a second search by a private contractor had to be ended with no success. Another search was done over 46,000 sq miles of seafloor down to southwest of Perth in Western Australia, yielded no evidence. Neither the crew nor the aircrafts communication system relayed a distress signal, bad weather was ruled out. Two Iranian passengers with stolen passport were eliminated as suspects. After clearing all the others, the Malaysian police identified the 53 year old pilot Captain Zaharie Ahmad Shah from Penang as prime suspect if human intervention was a possibility, although he had 18,365 hours of flying experience. With the loss of all 239 lives aboard flight 370 the passengers were from 14 different nations. The Boeing 777 was introduced in 1994 and has an excellent safety record. The Co-pilot was 27 year old Fariq Abdul Hamid who had 2763 hours of flying, also looked at but was eliminated as a suspect. Malaysia Airline sent immediate specially trained Buddhist counselors to Beijing and Malaysia to give emotional assistance to family members and friends. The planned flight duration was 5 hours and 34 minutes the aircraft carried 108,200 lb of jet fuel including reserves in addition to the passengers. In 2015 the US National Transportation Safety Board cited flight 370 when it issued eight new safety recommendations related to locating aircraft wreckage in remote or underwater location. The disappearance has been described as one of the biggest mysteries in modern aviation history. Malaysia Prime Minister Najib Razak said no place exist where it could have landed the aircraft therefore must have crashed into the sea.

INCA EMPIRE (603)

The Inca civilization rose from the Peruvian highlands sometime in the early 13th century. From about 1438 to 1533 they incorporated a large portion of western South America, primarily on the Andean Mountains. Unlike their Spanish neighbors the Inca's were peaceful people. They occupied Peru, Bolivia, Western Ecuador, and northwest Argentina the southwestern tip of Colombia, and large portions of Chile. Their official language was Quechua. They were smart people, their knowledge of iron and steel was monumental evidenced by their architecture, especially stone work, extensive road network reaching all corners of the empire. That was not all, finely woven textiles, use of knotted strings, their communication and agricultural innovations and production in a difficult environment as well as their organization, such as management and labor. They functioned largely without money and without markets, instead exchanged goods and services based on reciprocity between individuals, groups, and rulers. Taxes consisted of labor obligations their economy is a subject that requires some scholarly debates. They had many forms of worship most concerning local sacred Huacas although they worshipped Inti (their sun god) and imposed sovereignty above other cults such that of Pachamama, and considered their king the Sapa Inca the son of the sun. Although they were polytheists they worshipped many gods. There was a rain god, a hot tempered god causing earthquakes, a god of thunder and lightening, a fertility god, a moon god, a wisdom god, and many more; they believed in reincarnation. When the Spanish arrived to the Empire of the Incas they named it Peru, although the natives knew it as Tawantinsuyu. The Inca Empire was the last chapter of the Andean civilization they were a pastoral tribe in the Cusco area around the 12th century. The indigenous Peruvian oral history talks about three caves, four brothers and four sisters stepping out of these caves and their descendants were the ancestors of the Inca clans. It is a complicated story. They made human sacrifices; as many as 4,000 servants, court officials, and concubines were killed of the Inca Huayna Capac in 1527. They performed child sacrifices around important events such as the death of the Sapa Inca or during a famine. The Inca empire collapsed with arrival of the Spanish and as far as we know they have pretty much disappeared although it is believed that in the 13th and 14th century there might have been as many as 20 to 30 million Incas. Is there any connection between the Aztec and the Inca? We do not think so, the Aztec's were pushing south and the Incas moved northward, they were very different. There are few and may be none left of the Incas today, only God knows where they are.

HINDENBURG DISASTER (604)

LZ 129 Hindenburg was a German commercial <u>passenger-carrying-airship</u> of the Hindenburg class of flying machines, the largest airship by envelope volume, at the time designed and built by the Zeppelin Company in Germany. It was named after Field Marshal *Paul von Hindenburg*, who was president of Germany from 1925 until his death in 1934. The airship flew from March 1936 till May 1937 at which time it was destroyed by fire. It made 10 trips to the United States and a single round-trip from Frankford Germany to Rio de Janeiro Brazil. On 6 May, 1937, after crossing the Atlantic, the ship was in the process of landing at the Naval Air Station in Manchester New Jersey US with 97 people on board, when at 7.25 pm it caught fire and quickly became engulfed in flames, 35 people died, *(13 passengers and 22 crew)*, some survivors were severely burned. The flames quickly spread consuming 1 to 9 cells almost instantly, shooting a burst of flame out of the nose. The tail of the Hindenburg hit the ground first there was gas in the bow section of the ship pointing it upward while the rare section gravitated downward. There is wild speculation about what started the fire; a spark, a gas leak, static electricity, or the trail rope being overtightened. Unless you are building these machines it's really is not important how it started, we know the fire spread rapidly indicating that perhaps the builders of these ships need to find less flammable material to construct such vehicles in the future. There were many newsreels from media and some from surviving passengers. A film-clip was shown to Adolph Hitler in his bunker who watched it in stunned silence; it shattered public and industry faith in airship travel and contributed to the downfall of Zeppelins, but may have enhanced the arrival of Pan American Airlines. Hindenburg had offered more comfort to passengers, but Pan American offered speed. There were other airships built, but *Hindenburg* was leading the field of that class; its loss was catastrophic, but not the end of airships. The Zeppelin Company was not done yet and continued to explore other avenues. The disaster prompted the developers to look at all options and left no stone untouched. It may have ended Airship travel but opened other doors. Competition is a valuable ingredient in the world of research. Pan Am, KLM, and United are willing and capable to move people, so was the Queen Elizabeth. And Queen Mary. Hindenburg ended travel for some, but with advanced technology today, people can, (in the words of Josh Groban), "*dream the impossible dream and reach the unreachable star*" without ever stepping out of the house. Hindenburg & Titanic were tragic but life goes on.

SPRUCE GOOSE (605)

The Hughes H-4 Hercules aircraft, (Commonly known as the Spruce Goose) its owner was an eccentric millionaire named Howard Hughes. His interest was aviation and aerospace travel; in 1932 he formed Hughes Aircraft Company hiring numerous engineers, designers and defense contractors and in the 1930's and 40's he set multiple world air speed records. In 1942 the US War Department needed to transport battle material and personnel to Britain and this aircraft got their attention, it was the brainchild of Henry J. Kaiser, the leading Liberty Ship builder and manufacturer. Tanks, trucks and war machinery needed to be ferried across the Atlantic to Europe, at a time when The German U-boats had inflicted heavy losses on Allied Atlantic shipping traffic, the Spruce Goose which was the largest aircraft ever built, and Howard Hughes was called to testify before the Senate Investigative Committee and this is some of what he said: "*The Hercules was a monumental undertaking; it is the largest aircraft ever built it is over five stories tall with a wingspan longer than a football field. That is more than a city block. I put the sweat of my life into this thing. I have my reputation all rolled up in it and have stated several times if it's a failure I'll probably leave this country and never come back. And I mean it.*" Kaiser may have originated the idea of the flying ship, but he did not have an aeronautical background, therefore the partnership was great, but the project dragged on so long it frustrated Kaiser; delay was partly due to restriction on acquisition of certain materials, as well as the fact that Hughes insisted on perfection. After 16 months delay Kaiser withdrew from the project and Hughes continued on his own. A house moving company transported the airplane in three large sections to the Pier in Long Beach. A hangar was erected around the flying boat with a ramp to launch it in to the harbor. Tests and taxi runs were done with Hughes at the control it picked up speed at 135 mph and lifted to 70 ft high for about 1 mile and was airborne for 26 seconds, proving the plane was flight worthy, thus vindicating the use of government funds. After that it has never flown again, its lifting capacity was never tested; movie scenes from the Titanic were filmed there. A full time crew of 300 workers maintained the aircraft in flying condition in a climate controlled hangar, the crew was later reduced to 50 workers that was disbanded after Hughes died in 1976. In 1980 it was acquired by the Aero Club of Southern California which later put the aircraft on display in the Long Beach harbor next to the Queen Mary. Making it available for meetings, dinners and tours and has become a popular tourist attraction. We have not seen it as all of this took place after we moved away from Long Beach and return visits were too short and never went sightseeing.

ABORIGINAL PEOPLE (606)

Aboriginal people of the Australian mainland and many of the islands such as Tasmania, Fraser, Tiwi Island, and others have an air of mystery about them. There are many theories about their origin; one of them is they migrated from Southeast Asia by sea during the Pleistocene epoch, and lived over large sections of the continental shelf when Australia, Tasmania, and New Guinea when it was part of the same landmass known as Sahul. That may be so, but contemporary beliefs are still a complex mixture, varying by region and by individuals across Australia. Traditional cultural beliefs are passed down and shared by stories, art, dancing, and by an ancient creation known as dreaming when a spirit tells the humans to treat the animals and the earth with respect. The 2021 Census indicates that Aboriginals comprise 3,8% of Australia's 26 million people today most of them speak English, live in cities, and seem to have assimilated with the rest of Australia. A 2021 study by researchers of the Australian Research Council Centre of Excellence for Australian Biodiversity and Heritage has mapped the likely migration routes as they moved across the continent to its southern area known as Tasmania. This collective data from anthropologists, geomorphologists, climatologists, archeologists, ecologists, geneticists, hydrologists compared their findings of having studied and observed the linguistic features as well as their rock art. They possess inherited abilities to stand a wide range of environmental temperatures, can live comfortably through the heat of the desert and sleep soundly through a cold desert night. Aboriginals are genetically somewhat similar to the indigenous populations of Papua New Guinea and more distantly to groups of East Indonesia, distinct from indigenous people of Borneo and Malaysia, which may indicate that the Australian population likely has been isolated for a long time from the rest of Southeast Asia, even remained untouched by migrations. (*My only claim to fame about Australia is having visited there, and two of my New Zealand family resides there; otherwise my Australian wisdom is about as limited as any other*). Aboriginal Australians congregate mostly in remote areas of Australia, their communities experience a high rate of suicide especially among youth who feel disconnected from their culture; the murder rate of Aboriginal women, living on reservations, are ten times higher then the national average, making it the leading cause of death among the native population. Studies have revealed that they are genetically very different from the rest of the world, which makes them perhaps the most mysterious race of mankind.

MICRONESIA (607)

Micronesia is a sub-region of Oceania consisting of about 2,100 small islands in the Northwestern Pacific Ocean. The region has a tropical marine climate; it includes the Carolina Islands, the Gilbert Islands, the Mariana Islands, and the Marshall Islands as well as numerous other islands that are not part of any archipelago. Political control varies depending on the island. Some of the Carolina islands are part of Palau; some are part of the Federated States of Micronesia. The Gilbert Islands, (along with the Phoenix and the Line Islands in Polynesia) comprise of the Republic of Kribati. The Mariana Islands are affiliated with the US, some of them belong to the US Territory of Guam, and the rest belong to the US Commonwealth of the Northern Mariana Islands. The island of Nauru is its own sovereign nation. The Marshall Islands all belong to the Republic of the Marshall Islands. The sovereignty of Wake Island is contested; it is claimed by the United States and by the Republic of the Marshall Islands. The United States has actual possession of Wake Island which is under immediate administration of the United States Air Force. Human settlement of Micronesia began a long time ago some historians claim it was the BC Era perhaps 3000 to 1500 BCE. It is believed that from pre-Han Formosa Austronesians reached the northernmost Philippines as early as 2200 BCE and may have been the first people to have invented ocean going sailing technologies such as catamarans and outrigger boats. The earliest know contact of Europeans with Micronesia was in 1521, when

Magellan expedition landed in the Marianas. Jules Dumont d'Urville is usually credited with coining the term Micronesia in 1832, but in fact Louis Domeny de Rienzi used the term in 1831. Micronesia is a region in Oceania that includes approximately 2,100 islands with a total land area of 1,000 sq miles (2700 sq km)covering a total ocean area of about 2.9 million sq miles. The primary industry in Micronesia is fishing there is an abundance of open ocean there. They also enjoy the tourists but the industry is hampered by lack of infrastructure, which has quite a way to go, most tourists prefer a hotel room vs sleeping under a coconut tree or like a rental car to go site-seeing. According to Micronesia tourist bureau they get about 15,000 tourists a year. We have been tourists for many years and there is a certain amount of independence a tourist needs such as a hotel room a scooter, rental car, there is always an adequate supply of taxi's some quite reasonable, but we preferred our own wheels and explored the back roads. Micronesia exports coconuts, bananas, betel nuts. We would prefer the "*country*" atmosphere over infrastructure with unsophisticated environment get to know the local folks. We hope Micronesia will always be Micronesia.

MORANBONG BAND (608)

The Moranbong Band aka <u>Moran Hill Orchestra</u>), is a North Korean girl's band. The original members were selected by the countries supreme leader Kim Jung-Un; and the team performed interpretive styles of pop, rock, and fusion; the first such group making their world debut on 6 July 2012 appealing to the Western world with their varied musical style which was described as symphonic with harmonious pleasing result; it included Disney characters Mickey and Minnie Mouse, Snow white, Winnie the Pooh and a whole collection of World Fairy Tale Songs. The first performance raised hope now that the North Korea curtain had been raised proclaiming its birth to the world, resulting in South Korea media raised questions about a possible opening up of North Korea; but an official response came back from the north: "*There will be no policy shift as expected by enemy countries*." We can watch the band at home, as long as we are willing to endure military demonstrations; since the beginning the band's Western look has been toned down we can tune in as long as we will endure to see background filming of military parades and nuclear missiles showing the world, not just how talented North Korea's musicians are, but are reminded about display of NK military powers, something most western nations would not do. It is still fun to watch their show from time to time we can just ignore the parade of tanks. About that first show, one commentator wrote: ("If state propaganda is to be believed, the Moranbong Band's first performance is meant to stimulate production in the North

Korea textile sector…another commented…about the jewelry line up on the Moranbong singers…*The Korea Herald* reported about an scheduled tour which was cancelled because China requested that the Missiles not be shown during the performances one reviewer said; The Moranbong girls are not what you'd expect from an unfashionably totalitarian regime where grey is the new grey, their skirts are short, their hair is trendy, and the music danceable. It could pass as a Eurovision entry from Azerbaijan…") the band consists of only female musicians who play their own instruments and are talented. The band is quite large enabling them to play a variety of different styles of music as well as technically challenging arrangements. Members of the band hold high rankings in the military. In a concert in Pyongyang celebrating the start of 2019, without previous band leader Hyon Song-wol, a reviewer wrote The drastic changes in the musical composition of the songs has been interpreted to carry a message that rapid change is coming and things may end very differently than where they began. Knowing the history of the little fat boy and his sister in the north the report may be more real than not. Looking at North Korea we are not likely seeing a new policy in the north anytime soon.

MAYFLOWER (609)

A congregation of about 400 English protestants living in exile in Leiden Holland were dissatisfied with the reforms in the <u>Church of England</u> what they felt were abuses. With no success in making changes they chose to live separate in religiously tolerant Holland. They were illegal in England and when the authorities became aware of them they fled in the night with little more than the clothes they were wearing. After a while life became difficult in Holland often being engaged in open debates with leading theologians, as well as a brewing unrest of the fear that Spain might again place Holland under siege. They were called *Separatists* and became motivated with desires to set sail for the New World. It would be a major and risky undertaking; nevertheless they purchased two ships, the larger Mayflower and the smaller being the Speedwell, both were English ships that transported families known as Pilgrims to the New World. In 1620 the ships set sail but the Speedwell sprang a leak necessitating its return for repair, after three repairs 20 passengers were transferred to the overcrowded Mayflower, while the remainder returned to Holland. The Mayflower waited seven more days until the wind picked up in early September, by then western gales turned the North Atlantic into a dangerous place to sail. Now the Mayflower provisions were already quite low, even before the extra 20 came on; with all the delays the 102 passengers were very tired before the crossing could begin. Living quarters was cramped for the 102 passengers and 30 crew, in an area of 80 feet by 20 feet with a ceiling only 5 ft high. John Carver was called *the Moses of the Pilgrims*; and indeed it would require a Moses to keep the peace in such cramped quarters with many of them battling sea sickness emotions of all 130 people were tested to the max. After a grueling 10 weeks at sea, the gallant little craft eventually made it across and they reached the new world, (*now known as America or the United States*), it had carried the entire new congregation to a new nation, all of which were to begin anew in a less then friendly environment, while in search of a suitable settlement site. It was December and winter was coming, they were ill prepared for the bitter winter weather, in addition to the cold they faced starvation, were ill-clad in below freezing temperatures, with wet shoes and stockings that froze overnight, and lack of shelter. Over half of the new arrivals succumbed to Pneumonia, Tuberculosis, or just Exhaustion, before they even had a chance to settle and live their dream. With that in mind, we are first generation immigrants several centuries later; and wonder; why are our cities rioting? Why are they protesting and killing each other? Perhaps the Mayflower journey should be a required course in all schools.

TAJ MAHAL (610)

The Taj Mahal was built in 1631 by Shah Jahan in memory of his wife Mumtaz Mahal who died 17 June of that year while giving birth to their 14th child Gauhara Begum. Construction on the mausoleum began the following year which employed some 20,000 artisans under the guidance of a board of architects at a cost of around 32 million rupees, estimated at about 35 billion in today's money. 1,000 elephants were used to transport building materials from all over India and Asia. Some 22,000 laborers, painters, embroidery artists and stone cutters were used. The translucent white marble was brought from Makrana, Rajasthan, the jasper from the Punjab region, jade and crystal from China. Turquoise from Tibet, and Lapis lazuli from Afghanistan, sapphire from Sri Lanka, and the carnelian from Arabia. In all 28 types of precious stone were inlaid into the white marble. It is said that Shah Jahan decreed that anyone could keep the brick taken from the scaffold, and thus it was dismantled by peasants overnight. In 1983 it was designated as a UNESCO World Heritage for being the jewel of Muslim Art in India, and is one of the universally admired masterpieces of the world's heritage. It is regarded by many as the best example of Mughal architecture and a symbol of India's rich history. The Taj Mahal has attracted more than 6 million visitors a year and in 2007 it was declared a winner of the new 7 wonders of the world (2000-2007) initiative. Along with being a symbol of love it is also a symbol of Shah Jahan's wealth and power, and the fact that the empire had prospered under his rule. From the structure as well as the gardens it is a paradise on earth. Eleanor Roosevelt commented, the white symbolized the purity of real love. The Tas Mahal is often seen as a feminine architectural form in the Islamic world is even thought by some to embody Mumtaz Mahal herself. They had other family issues of which I know nothing about, after all it was in the 1600's and time is marching on. Some News articles have referred to the fact that soon after the Taj Mahal completion, Shah Jahan was deposed by his son Aurangzeb and put under house arrest at the nearby Agra Fort, from where he could see the Taj Mahal. Upon Shah Jahan's death, Aurangzeb buried him in the mausoleum next to his wife. In the 18th century, Jat rulers invaded Agra and attacked the Taj Mahal they took away 2 chandeliers one of agate and another of silver, they also took the gold and silver screen. By the late 19th century some of the buildings had fallen into disrepair, at that time British viceroy Lord Curzon ordered a sweeping restoration which was completed in 1908. The garden was modeled with European style lawns, most are still in place today. Pollution has been turning the Taj Mahal yellow brown, the India Supreme Court has issued directives.

MACCABEES (611)

Maccabees aka First book of Maccabees is a deuterocanonical book which details the history of the Maccabean revolt against the Seleucid Empire as well as the history of the Hasmonean Kingdom. The time period referred here is from around 170 BC to 134 BC, or for those of us who are Christian it is the period between the Old Testament and the New Testament. Protestants do not have the books of the Maccabees in their Bible, but the Roman Catholic Bible includes seven more intertestament books including those of the Maccabees. Protestant Bibles have 39 books in the Old Testament and Catholics have 46, among them are the Maccabees, and five others. Until the 16th century most Christians accepted the older <u>Alexandrian canon</u>, (*list of inspired books*), <u>until</u>, and <u>when</u>, Martin Luther translated the Bible into the German language, and being the Scholar that he was with his PhD in Bible (*he threw a monkey ranch in there*), and did not think seven of the old Testament books should be on equal footing with the rest of the inspired books of the Bible, that would include the Maccabee books. We had a Bible in our home with the extra seven books that were referred to as the "*<u>Apocrypha</u>*". In 1546 the Council of Trent did not agree with Luther and decreed that these seven books must be accepted and remain in the Bible. In relation to that, this might interest you: After the Jerusalem Temple was destroyed, the rabbis of rabbinic Judaism, accepted as inspired only books written in Hebrew. The Alexandrian canon contains seven books written in Greek, and parts of two others. The author of 1 Maccabees is unknown, and written in post-independence of the Hasmonean kingdom, probably during the reign of high Priest John Hyrcanus (134-104 BC), most agree that the book was written before 63 BC as the author shows great admiration toward Rome, but was not aware of Roman general Pompey conquering Jerusalem reducing the Hasmonean kingdom to a client state of Rome in that year. He may be some kind of court historian, it was evident that he was aware of Judea and its geography, but seems less informed about the wider Hellenistic world. The book could have been written in Greek or Hebrew; historians who have studied that era generally agree that the entire account is most likely composed by one author. The word Maccabee only refers to Judah. It was not used in plural *Maccabees* till years later when describing the martyrs; it seems to have been written in Judea where the knowledge of Greek & Hebrew was more widespread. The English equivalent would be like writing new books today in the style of the King James, even if Luther thought they should not be included with the inspired Bible books they are certainly great historical reading of the Hasmonean days.

SPECIAL OLYMPICS (612)

Special Olympics is the world's largest sports organization for children and adults with intellectual disabilities providing year-round training and activities to 5 million participants and unified sports partners in 172 countries. Competitions are held every day, all around the world including national and regional competitions, adding up to more than 100,000 events a year. It is recognized by the International Olympic Committee. The world games are a major event and alternate between winter and summer games. The first one was held July 20, 1968 in Chicago with 1,000 athletes from the US and Canada, and was chaired by Eunice Kennedy Shriver. Participation has expended in subsequent games. In 2003 the first summer games held outside the US were in Dublin Ireland with 7000 athletes from 150 countries. In 2019 the games were held in Abu Dhabi, United Arab Emirates and 2023 games were held in Berlin Germany. The first winter Games were held in 1977 in Steamboat Springs Colorado. Austria held one in 2017. What is the qualification for Special Olympics? **1**: Intellectual disability **2**: Slow learning determined by standardized measures **3**: significant vocational problems resulting from cognitive delay. Must be eight years old, male or female, defined by American Association on mental retardation, intellectual functioning two years behind peers, limited in adaptive skills such as communication, self care, home living, social skills, health and safety, children with Down syndrome, much of the time are already in special education programs. We dealt with it in the Foster Care program. The goal of Special Olympics is to help bring all persons with intellectual disability in to the larger society under conditions whereby they are accepted and respected, and encourage the athlete to move from Special Olympics to compete in regular sports activity, this is always the athlete's choice. Its goal is to enhance their dignity and self esteem. Participation in the training programs is open to those of age 8 and higher. Comprehensive year around training is conducted by well-qualified coaches in accordance with standardized sports rules formulated by Special Olympics. Every Special program includes sports events; every award ceremony will have 1st 2nd and 3rd places with suitable ribbons and medals. Preferably coaches will be local volunteers. To offer athletes a full range of artistic, social and cultural experiences through activities such a dances, art exhibits, concerts, visits to historic sites, clinics, theatrical performances and similar activities. The spirit of Special Olympics incorporates skill, courage, sharing and joy. These are universal values which transcend boundaries of geography.

POMPEII (613)

Pompeii was an ancient city located near Naples in the Campania region of Italy. Pompeii along with Herculaneum was buried under 4 to 6 m (13-20 ft) of volcanic ash in the Eruption of Mount Vesuvius in 79 AD. Largely preserved under the ash, the excavated city offers a unique snapshot of Roman life frozen at the moment it was buried, although quite a bit was lost during the excavation. It was a wealthy town with a population of about 11,000 enjoying many fine public buildings and luxurious private homes with lavish decorations, furnishings and works of art. There is some indication of post eruption disturbance when thieves came to salvage valuables including jewelry, even statutes and other pieces of building materials indicative of the fact that after the ash had settled people went in there to enrich themselves. Over time human bodies interred in the ash decayed, leaving voids that archeologists could not use as moulds to make plaster casts of figures in their final moments of life. Pompeii has become a UNESCO World Heritage Site and is one of the most popular tourist attractions in Italy, with about 2.5 million visitors annually. Many excavations were made prior to 1960 that uncovered most of the city, but left it in decay. Pompeii was built approximately 130 ft above sea level on a coastal lava plateau created by earlier eruptions of Mount Vesuvius. The city once by the shoreline of the Mediterranean, is today 2300 ft inland; Pompeii covered an area of about 170 acres and was home to approximately 11,000 people based on household counts. In about 64, Nero and his wife Poppaea, visited Pompeii and made offerings at the temple of Venus the city's deity. Some historians have estimated that by 79 the population might have been as high as 20,000, but more recent estimates are 11,000 based on household counts. The eruption lasted for two days, or approximately 18 hours, around 1,150 bodies or remains, have been discovered at the site, many still wearing their Jewelry while some had coins or silverware, which indicates that this eruption must have been a pyroclastic flow consisting of scorching hot ash clouds hotter then boiling water hitting the city at high speed leaving the whole area buried under 15 to 20 ft of ash; it is believed that the main cause of death was heat. The time of the year was determined by the clothes people were wearing. Pompeii was known to be an affluent city. (A more *recent example of a pyroclastic eruption accident was in Japan on 3 June 1991 when 33 year old American volcanologist Harry Glicken 'who had escaped death at Mount St Helen' when, along with 37 others were engulfed and killed in seconds at Mount Unzen by one such eruption).*

MOUNT RAINIER (614)

Mount Rainier is a large active stratovolcano in the cascade range of the Pacific Northwest located in the Mount Rainier national park in the US State of Washington. It has a summit elevation of 14,417 ft, making it the highest mountain in the US. Due to its high probability of an eruption in the near future in is considered one of the most dangerous volcanoes in the world; about 80,000 people and their homes are at risk in Mount Rainier's lahar hazard zones. While visiting friends in Naches having driven around it to Yakima taking the freeway and returning to Seattle taking the back on the mountain road, I never realized till now, that we drove around the most dangerous mountain three different times. Between 1950 and 2018, 439,460 people have climbed the mountain and from 1947 to 2018, 84 people have died in various mountain accidents. The diverse indigenous people who have lived in the vicinity for many generations have many names for the mountain in their various languages. George Vancouver named it honor of his friend, Rear Admiral Peter Rainier. The map of Lewis & Clark refers to it as Mt. Regniere, Theodore Winthrop referred to the mountain as Tacoma. Names have been used interchangeably although the residents of the nearby city of Tacoma prefer that name. In 1890, the United States Board on Geographic names declared that the mountain should be known as Rainier. In 1897, the Pacific Forest Reserve became the Mount Rainier Forest Reserve and the National Park was established three years later. And became the Mount Rainier

Forest Reserve; the National Park was established later. The size of glaciers has fluctuated over the years from 25,000 in the last ice age to 15,000 what it is now. The glaciers are inside the boundaries of Mount Rainier and lost volume in the last decades and have been thinning and retreating according to a study using data from 1980 to 2021. These glaciers can generate mudflows. At one time the river valleys and other areas near the mountain we inhabited by native Americans who hunted and gathered animals and plants in Mount Rainier's forests and high elevation meadows. Modern reprentatives of these tribes and the human use of these mountains date back thousands years. Some these natives have been setting fire to some areas to encourage meadow development. The first Europeans to reach the Pacific Northwest arrived by sea; upon landing the crew was attacked and killed by the local indigenous population, therefore it is possible that the Spanish sailors may have first discovered Mount Rainier, but did not live long enough to record it.

TROJAN HORSE (615)

The story of The Trojan Horse came to us as babies and we wanted to hear about it over and over; it was about a wooden horse said to have been used by the Greeks during the Trojan War to enter the city of Troy and win the war. After a fruitless 10-year siege the Greeks constructed a huge wooden horse, and hid a select force of men inside including Odysseus himself. The Greeks pretended to sail away, and the Trojans pulled the horse in the city as a trophy. That night the Greeks crept out of the horse and opened the gates for the rest of the Greek army which had sailed back under the cover of darkness, the Greek army entered and destroyed the city, ending the war. Metaphorically, a "*Trojan Horse*" has come to mean any trick or stratagem that causes a target to invite foe into a securely protected bastion or place. A malicious computer program that tricks users into willingly running it is also called a "*Trojan horse*". Odysseus was the chief architect of the project. In the Greek tradition the horse is called the wooden horse. Thirty of their best warriors and two spies hid inside the wooden horse. The story is also alluded to in Greek classical literature. Animal names are often used for military machinery which was often covered with dampened horse hides to protect against flaming arrows. Pasusanias, who lived in the 2nd century AD, wrote in his book: "That the work of Epeius was a contrivance to make breach in the Trojan wall is known to everybody who does not attribute utter silliness to the Phrygians" by the Phrygians, he meant the Trojans. Some authors have suggested that the gift might also have been a ship, with warriors hidden inside. It has been noted that the terms used to put men in the horse are those used by ancient Greek authors to describe the embarkation of men on a ship and that there are analogies between the building of ships by Paris at the beginning of the Trojan saga and the building of a the horse at the end; ships are called "sea horses" once in the *Odyssey*. This view has gained support from Naval archaeology; ancient text and images show that a Phoenician merchant ship type decorated with a horse head, called hippos (horse) by Greeks, became very diffuse in the Levant area around the beginning of the first millennium BC and was used to trade precious metal and sometimes to pay tribute after the end of a war. It caused the suggestion that the original story viewed the Greek soldiers hiding inside the hull of such a vessel and might have been misunderstood in the oral transmission of the story. There is no shortage of Trojan horse stories some more speculative then others. Whether true or myth these stories bring great imagination to the minds of children it did to us; Einstein said: "Imagination is more important than knowledge, for knowledge is limited, but imagination embraces the entire world".

OTTOMAN EMPIRE (616)

The Ottoman Empire is generally understood to be the Turkish Empire that controlled much of Southeast Europe, Western Asia, and Northern Africa from the end of the 13th century till and when the Ottoman military system began to weaken against its rivals the Habsburg and Russian Empire, and suffered severe military defeats in the late 18th and early 19th centuries it was then that the crumbling became inevitable. The word Ottoman is a historical Anglicization of the name Ossma-1 who is considered the founder of the Empire and the ruling House of Osman (aka) the Ottoman dynasty. The Turkish word for Ottoman (Osmanh) originally referred to the tribal followers of Osman in the 14th century, and after his death began to extend over Anatolia and the Balkans, everything went smooth until the earliest conflicts began during the Byzantine–Ottoman-wars in the late 13th century going into the 14th century followed by the Bulgarian-Ottoman wars and the Serbian-Ottoman conflicts. The port city of Thessaloniki (aka Thessalonica), was captured from the Venetians in 1387 paving the way for the Ottoman Empire to expand into Europe. The successful Greek war of Independence concluded with decolonization of Greece following the London Protocol (1830) and Treaty of Constantinople (1832). This and other defeats prompted the Ottoman state to initiate a comprehensive process of reform and modernization known as *Tanzimat*, which made them more powerful, despite suffering some territorial losses especially in the Balkans. Tanzimat has been the subject of quite a bit of controversy; it is always difficult to guess intentions; some have claimed it was just to get European diplomatic support at a very critical time, it may also have something to do with the forthcoming reform announcements, we may never know, especially in light of the fact that Tanzimat has been the subject of much misconception. The Committee of Union and Progress (CUP) in 1908 turned the Empire into a constitutional monarchy which conducted competitive multi-party elections. After the disastrous Balkan war, and the 1913 *coup d'etat,* CUP took over the government especially the result became a one-party regime. From 1914 to 1918 Europe battled WW-I, and the CUP allied the empire with Germany which contributed to territorial losses, even though the empire was holding its own, they struggled with internal dissent especially with the Arab Revolt in its Arabian holdings. The successful Turkish war of Independence led to the emergence of the Republic of Turkey in the Anatolian heartland and the abolition of the Ottoman monarchy. Perhaps the Ottoman is like all other empires, which eventually crumble and/or dissolve.

VANUATU (617)

The Republic of Vanuatu is a French island in the South Pacific Ocean in a volcanic archipelago that is located 1090 mi east of northern Australia, east of New Guinea, and west of Fiji. The first Europeans, the Spanish, arrived in 1606, led by Portuguese navigator Fernandes de Queiros, who claimed the archipelago for Spain. A few centuries later, in 1880, France and the United Kingdom claimed it, they called it New Hebrides; then in 1970 the local people wanted independence, resulting in the fact that the Republic of Vanuatu was founded 10 years later in 1980 which is now a member of the United Nations. The early history of Vanuatu is not to clear due to the fact that nothing was written; people relied on oral transmission of their own history which often gets lost and over time is subject to misunderstanding, therefore one has to dig deep; in more recent times some archeological research has been done, they have excavated ancient burial sites, conducted most notably at Teouma on Efate where there is a large ancient Cemetary. The Lapita sites became Vanuatu's first UNESCO World Heritage site in 2008. The immediate origins of the Lapita lay to the northwest, in the Solomon Islands and the Bismark Archipelago of Papua New Guinea, though DNA studies of century's old skeleton indicate some may have come from the Philippines and/or Taiwan and may have brought with them crops such as Yam, Taro, and Banana as well as Pigs & Chickens. Their arrival is coincident with the extinction of several species, such as land crocodiles, land tortoise and various bird species. Lapita settlements reached as far east as Tonga and Samoa. Over time the Lapita culture lost much of its early unity and became increasingly fragmented the precise reason is unclear. Over time it is thought that the Lapita likely mixed with the other races from Bismark or Melanesia, ultimately producing the darker-skinned physiognomy that is quite typical in Ni-Vanuatu; linguistically the Lapita peoples'Austronesian languages are maintained quite well. Europeans did not return till 1768 when French explorer Louis Antoine de Bougainville sailed by the islands 22 May; at first they were trading but then got attacked. James Cook came by there in 1774 and named them New Hebrides. Whaling-ships were among the first regular visitors in 1804 and from 1839 onwards missionaries Roman Catholic and Protestant, arrived in the island; at first they faced hostility, most notably with the killings of John Williams and James Harris of the London Missionary society in 1839. The Anglican Church took young Melanesian converts for training to New Zealand. Presbyterians were also quite successful; although all missionaries were repeatedly chased of the island by locals throughout the 1840's to 1860's some due to the fact that they brought inadvertently illness and death.

PENTAGON (618)

The Pentagon is the headquarters building of the United States Department of Defense, in Arlington Virginia across the Potomac River in Washington DC. The building was designed by American Architect George Bergstrom and built by contractor John McCain. It was constructed in World War II from 11 Sept. 1941 until it was finished and dedicated on 15 Jan. 1943. It is the world's largest office building with about 6.5 million sq.ft (150 acres) of floor space. Some 23,000 military and civilian employees, and another 3,000 non-defense support personnel, work in the pentagon. It has five sides, five floors above ground, two basement levels and five ring corridors per floor which comes to a total of 17.5 mi of corridors. The building spans 28.7 acres and includes an additional 5.1 acres as a central courtyard. It cost $31, 1 million, (in today's money about $446 million). Starting on the north side and moving clockwise, its five façade entrances are the Mall Terrace, the River Terrace, the Concourse, the South parking, and the Heliport. On one of my visits to the Nations Capital, we were asked one morning if any of us would like to visit the pentagon tomorrow or rather enjoy a free day. Ten of us raised our hand; "We chipped in a little money and rented a van with driver, upon boarding the next morning the driver said I am new here, I hope we find it. It was before phone navigation devises. None of us knew the way; I sat near the front and asked: we have been twice around it, should we not go inside? He said: I know, every time I think we go in we are led out again, he stopped the van and said: You better get off here while we can still see it; it was a clear morning and good fresh walk. Going in, we were invited inside the office of the Secretary of defense for an early Morning Prayer meeting, it was impressive. I counted 16 men with the rank of General or Admiral, all being there in uniform for the early Morning Prayer meeting bowing our knees before a Holy God, at the beginning of the workday. It was an impressive meeting, after which we were given a tour of the building. My heart went back to my younger days where such leaders bowed before Hitler as their god. This was America and as an immigrant here I thought: <u>what a country</u>! The guided tour of the Pentagon was worth it. Later the building was substantially damaged in the 11 September al-Qaeda hijackers attack when they flew American Airlines flight 77 into the building killing themselves and 184 others, 59 on the plane and 125 in the Pentagon; it was the first significant foreign attack on government facilities in Washington DC since the British attack of 1812 setting several buildings on fire in Washington. Four days after that, the Lord intervened with a heavy thunderstorm a massive downpour which extinguished the fires.

BATAAN MARCH (619)

The Bataan March of April 1942 during World War II in the Philippenes has also been referred to as the Death March. It began on 9 April 1942 after the three month battle of Bataan in the Philippines during World War II; and became a forcible transfer by the Imperial Japanese Army of 75,000 American and Filipino prisoners of war (POW) on the Bataan Peninsula to Camp O'Donnell via San Fernando. The total distance was about 65 miles (105 km), although reports varied, upon reaching Camp O'Donnell it was estimated that from 5,000 to 18,000 Filipinos died, and about 500 to 650 Americans died during the march, which has been characterized by *the* worst brutality in that war. One POW had a beautiful ring, the guard said take it off but it was hard to come off and the guard took out a machete and cut the men's wrist off took the ring leaving him bleeding profusely and stuck a bayonet in the stomach. At the beginning there were rare instances of kindness of Japanese officers some of who spoke English, such as sharing food or cigarettes, but as time went on and fatigue set in the soldiers grew impatient and greedier, even knocking out teeth to get the gold fillings. One of the major massacres was attributed to Colonel Masanobu Tsuji when 400 Filipino officers under his supervision were massacred in the Pantingan River after they had surrendered. No food or water was given during the march to the POW's, some were forced to strip naked and sit in sweltering direct sunlight without head covering even within sight of fresh cool water. If they succumbed to fatigue, trucks ran over them and/or randomly soldiers would stab the POW with bayonets. The march had a large impact on New Mexico, given that many of the America soldiers came from there, specifically from the 200th and 515th Coast Guard Artillery of the National Guard; they organized the Bataam Memorial Museum. The old state capital building of New Mexico was renamed the Bataan Memorial Building and now houses several state government agency offices. The main force had been that of General Masaharu Homma who came ashore when the defenders failed to hold the beaches. He encountered twice as many captives as he had estimated and was faced with moving 60,000 starved, sick, and debilitated, prisoners that were caught in the battle; the soldiers began with shaking down all POW's and confiscate their valuables even forcibly removed gold teeth, then were ordered to march 65 miles to the next destination under inhumane brutalities. After WW-II these leaders were tried and convicted. Major General Yoshitaka Kawane and Colonel Kurataro Hirano were sentenced to death by hanging and executed at Sugamo Prison, some received the firing squad.

SEXTANT (620)

A sextant is a navigation instrument that measures the angular distance between two visible objects. The primary use of a sextant is to measure the angle between an astronomical object and the horizon for the purpose of celestial navigation. The estimation of this angle, the altitude, is known as *sighting* or *shooting* the object, or *taking a sight*. The angle, and the time when it was measured, can be used to calculate a position line on a nautical or aeronautical chart-for example, sighting the Sun at noon or Polaris at night (in the Northern Hemisphere) to estimate latitude (with sight reduction). Sighting the height of a landmark can give a measure of *distance off* and, held horizontally; a sextant can measure angles between objects for a position on a chart. It can also be used to measure the lunar distance between the moon and another celestial object (such as a star or a planet). The principle of the instrument was first implemented around 1731 by John Hadley and Thomas Godfrey, but it was also found later in the unpublished writings of Isaac Newton (1643-1727. In 1922, it was modified for aeronautical navigation by Portuguese navigator and naval officer Gago Coutinho. Like the Davis quadrant, the sextant allows celestial objects to be measured relative to the horizon, rather than relative to the instrument. It allows excellent precision. Also, unlike the backstaff, the sextant allows direct observation of stars. This permits the use of the sextant at night when the backstaff is difficult to use. For solar observation filter need be used to observe the sun; most sextants have filters for use when viewing the sun and reducing the effects of haze. The filters usually consist of a series of progressively dark glasses that can be used singly or in combination to reduce haze and the sun's brightness. However, sextants with adjusting polarizing filters have also been manufactured where the degree of darkness is adjusted by twisting the frame of the filter. A sextant does not require a completely steady aim, such as when on a moving ship, the image of both horizon and celestial object will move around in the field of view. An artificial horizon is useful when the horizon is invisible, as occurs in fog, on moonless nights when sighting through a window or on land surrounded by trees or buildings. There are two common designs of artificial horizon. It can consist simply of a pool of water shielded from the wind, allowing the user to measure the distance between the body and its reflection, and divide by two. Another design allows the mounting of a fluid-filled tube with bubble directly to the sextant. Most sextants mount a 1 or 3-power monocular for viewing. A change in temperature can warp the arc, creating inaccuracies many navigators purchase waterproof cases so that their sextant can be placed outside the cabin to come to equilibrium with outside temperatures.

CREMATION (621)

Cremation is a method of final disposition of a dead body through burning. It leaves about 5 lbs of ashes that do not constitute any health risk whether retained by relatives, interred in a memorial site, or scattered in various ways. (*Here in Hawaii it's common to scatter at sea*). Burial or cremation differs based on religious practice; the choice is generally left to the family, who historically debated the issue. In the Middle East and Europe there is much archeological evidence that both were practiced throughout the years. Cultural groups have had serious disagreement on both issues; the ancient Egyptians developed an intricate transmigration-of-soul theology which prohibited cremation; the Babylonians, according to Herodotus, embalmed their dead, Phoenicians practiced both cremation and burial. Greeks practiced burial. In Rome's early history, both inhumation and cremation were common among all. In Europe, there are traces of cremation, date to the Early Bronze Age (*3300-1200 BC*) the custom became dominant at that time. Europe practiced the Urn field culture (*1300-750 BCE*). In the Iron Age inhumation again became more common, but cremation persisted in the Villanovan culture. Hinduism and Judaism are noted for not only allowing, but prescribing, cremation. In India it's first attested in the Cemetary H culture as far back as *1900 BCE*. Cremation remained common but not universal, in both ancient Greece and ancient Rome. According to Cicero, burial was considered an archaic rite in Rome. The rise of Christianity saw cremation coming to an end in Europe, although it was already in decline. In early Roman-Britain, cremation was usual but diminished by the 4th century. It then reappeared in the 5th and 6th centuries during the migration era even sacrificed animals were sometimes included in the pyre. That custom was also widespread among the Germanic peoples of the northern continental lands from which the Anglo-Saxon migrants are supposed to have been derived during that period. The ashes were usually deposited in a vessel of clay or bronze and placed in an "urn cemetery". The custom again died out with the Christian conversion of the Anglo-Saxons or Early English during the 7th century, when Christian burial became general; at that time in some parts of Europe cremation was forbidden by law, even punishable by death if combined with Heathen rites, although it was often approved by Catholic authorities as part of punishment for accused heretics such as burning at the stake. For example the body of John Wycliffe was exhumed years after his death and burned with ashes thrown in the river as punishment for denying the doctrine of transubstantiation; as far as we can determine the Bible has no comment for or against cremation, may be a deeper study of Genesis 3:19, Job 30:19, and Ecclesiastes 3:20 is helpful.

AMISH (622)

The early Amish history is rooted in the days of Huldrych Zwingli (*1484-1531*), who led the Reformation in Switzerland. It was the Anabaptist movement of Lord Zinzendorf, from which the Amish later emerged. (Luther's following was mostly in Germany, Calvin's in France and Holland), and Zwingli's primarily in Switzerland, there was a cost, for many it was their life. Amish life began with adult baptism, then being hunted by the Roman Church, by the Turks, even some Reformers, and by the government _which was the Roman church, both were the same_. Their leader Zwingli was a chaplain in the war; he picked up the sword and died by the sword. He fought in the First Kappel War against the church who hunted him down. It was in the early morning of 11 Oct. 1531 when the first rays of the morning sun filtered through the dew laden pine trees when an angry and hungry army of several thousand man crossed into Protestant Zurich; Ulrich Zwingli mounted his horse and rode out to meet the enemy he shouted they want blood, as blasting muskets, groaning men and screaming horses, Zwingli shouted they can kill the body but not the soul. He encouraged his men, but before the day was over Ulrich Zwingli met his maker. (After Wycliffe, Hus and Tyndale he was the first major reformer to die, Luther Calvin & Knox died a few years later). (This is fascinating history, and w*hile meeting in Geneva, I took a few hour train ride to Zurich, found his massive cathedral, visible from anywhere in the city, the church door was open I got inside, was alone and climbed* *in Zwingli's pulpit and stood there several minutes imagining how he must have felt when standing here encouraging his followers to be faithful to the Savior till the end, he knew they could be martyrs at any moment; standing where he had stood in his pulpit on that early morning was an emotional experience I will not forget."* To be an Amish member, meant you would not ever own an automobile, phone, use electricity, and resign to a simple life, practice none-resistance, perform no military service. They migrated from Europe to Pennsylvania in the 18th century; more came in the 19th century. In World War-II the draft kept surfacing. (*I served in the 1950's in the Marine Corps; military service was required. I served quite happy for a few years*). What about the Amish? A compromise was reached; we were sent overseas to fight wars, the Amish men were required to give 2 or 3 years in public service such as forestry, or work in hospitals. While America is advancing more into technology, quite a few Amish youth have abandoned *horse and buggy life*, they now own laptops, automobiles, cell-phones, use electricity and begin to assimilate! Having said that, there are some plusses to living a simplistic and isolated life which some of us, (who are a little older), have abandoned.

YAP (623)

Yap, (Sometimes written as Wa'ab), refers to an island group located in the Carolina islands of the western Pacific Ocean. It is made up of four separate islands: <u>Yap Proper</u>, <u>Gagil-Tamil</u>, <u>Maap</u>, and <u>Rumung</u>; the four islands are encircled by a common coral reef, separated by relatively small water features, Gagil-Tamil and Yap Proper were once linked, but in 1901 a narrow canal called *Tagireeng-Canal* was built to cut the two landmasses apart. Yap was formed from an uplift of the Philippine Sea Plate and is referred to as a high island, as opposed to atolls; the climate is tropical the land consists mostly of rolling hills with densely vegetated valleys and savanna interiors, with Mangrove swamps lining much of the shore, although there are beaches on the northern and western sides of the islands. The main Yap Islands are about 24 km long and 5-10 km wide. Mount Taabiywol, the highest mountain, on Yap Proper is elevated 178 m (584 ft); about 11,500 people, divided into ten municipalities, live in Yap islands. At one time the inhabitants were hostile from time to time. There is no gold or silver on Yap but the money consists of large carved limestone deposits, some weigh more then a car. It is not clear when *that* practice started; these stones are their version of gold, it was their money. A piece of stone was really valuable, although not used for day to day money, more suitable for special transaction like a daughter's dowry. Ownership of a stone changes after a transaction, but all residents know who owns it even though the stone was not moved. A work crew brought a giant stone to Yap in a canoe, the boat capsized and the stone descended to the bottom of the ocean. It's been there for 100 years, no one has seen it, but it's still valid money today, and it is used in trading. Disks are no longer produced or imported; every one in the village knows who at any given time owns a particular stone, even though ownership changes with marriage, death, land deals. Yap has three types of buildings. The _tabinaw_, is a family home, it has one large room no lavatory, and no kitchen. Another building was the _faluw_, the men's house; often the most beautiful women lived there, but that practice has ended. A third structure is the _p'ebay_, it's for meetings, school, or festivities. Austronesian is the Yap language somewhat similar to the Solomon Islands, or New Guinea. Yap is preserving the culture by mixing the old with the new. The people are not simply dropping their culture, but maintain their traditions and can boast about the most intact culture in all Micronesia; from the taro patch to the government offices, the community is able to function in a mixed world with cultural traditions, and still live in the 21st century; _that_ is the Yap miracle.

YANGTZE RIVER (624)

The Yangtze River is the longest river in Eurasia, and is the third longest in the world and is the longest in one country, all of the 6,300 km (3,915 mi), is within the borders of China; (having said that, measuring the length of a river is not an exact science, for example, there is still disagreement among scientists whether the Nile or the Amazon is the world's longest river), the official Chinese name in Mandarin is "_Long River_." Marco Polo called the river Quian or Quianshui, the name he used putting it on the map. During the 18th century some referred to it as the Blue River as opposed to the other one which was the Yellow River that was running south. The Yangtze River has played a major role in the historic culture and economy of China. It originates from several tributaries in the eastern part of the Tibetan Plateau, two of which are commonly referred to as the source, although the Chinese government has recognized the Tuotuo tributary, which is at the base of a glacier lying on the west of Geladandong Mountain in the Tanggula Mountains. The true source of the Yangtze, (hydrologically the longest river distance from the sea), is Jari Hill at the head of the Dam Qu tributary approximately 325 km (202 mi) southeast of Geladandong. All these tributaries join as the river runs eastward through Quinghai (Tsinghai), then turning south to Sichuan; (it was there in Panda country that I met the Yangtze River), in the course of this valley, where it drops from above 16.000 ft to 3,300 ft. The River has been used for water, transportation, war, irrigation, sanitation, boundary-marking, and other useful purposes. The prosperous Yangtze Delta generates as much as 20% of China's GDP. The Three Gorges Dam is the largest hydro-electric power station in the world that is in use. The river flows through a wide array of ecosystems and is habitat to several threatened species including the Chinese Alligator, the Yangtze Sturgeon, the narrow ridged finless Porpoise, and the now extinct Yangtze River Dolphin, which is extinct in the wild. In recent years the river has suffered from industrial pollution, as well as tourist pollution such as plastic, and also agricultural runoff, siltation, and the loss of wetland and lakes, which exacerbates seasonal flooding. Some sections of the river are now protected as nature reserves by UNESCO World Heritage Sites. Some sections of the Yangtze River have local names. From Yibin to Yichang, running through Sichuan and Ghongging municipality it is known as the Chuan Jiang or as the Sichuan River. Four of China's five main freshwater lakes contrite their waters to the Yangtze River, after entering Hubei province the Yangtze receives water from quite few sources. Where Lake Poyang meets the river; the downstream part is from Hukou to Shanghai.

GREAT WALL OF CHINA (625)

The Great Wall of China goes back to the years from the 8th to the 5th century BC, and the period of wars between Qin, Han, and Zhongshan dynasties when construction of the wall was begun for purpose to defend a fortified border. It was built to withstand attacks of small arms such as swords and spears. Our guide took us to a spot outside Peking where we got on the wall and hike to a plateau; it was a clear day and we could see much of the wall ahead. King Zheng of Qin conquered the last of his opponents and unified China in 221 BC as the Qin dynasty intended to impose centralized rule, he ordered the destruction of some sections of the wall. We were advised the wall is currently 21 km (13 mi), although in China it is referred to as ten thousand mile. A traditional Chinese mile varied with terrain and was often based on the size of a village. Today, the *Great Wall* is generally recognized as one of the most impressive architectural feats in history, and is titled one of the 7 wonders of the world it took several centuries to construct. Apart from defense, the Great Wall has functioned as border control, imposition of duties on goods transported along the Silk Road, regulation on trade, and control of immigration. Strength of the wall was enhanced by the construction of watchtowers, troop's barracks, and signaling capabilities by means of smoke or fire. The path along the Great Wall served as transportation corridor. Because of the wall's association with the First Emperor's tyranny, the Qin dynasty, locals referred to it as the "*Long*

Wall". Transporting large quantities of materials up and down mountains was difficult, therefore builders used local resources such as stones from the mountains; rammed earth was used for constructing foundations; (*Rammed earth was a damp mixture of subsoil, gravel, clay, silt, sand and stabilizer such as lime and/ or animal blood to stabilize it*), the mix was poured into a form work 4 x 10 inch mixed, and used for the foundation on which a stone wall is erected. (*In modern days walls are constructed on top of footings or on a reinforced concrete slab base*). Most of the ancient Qin walls have eroded away over the centuries, and very few sections remain today. The human cost of construction is not known but it has been estimated by some authors that hundreds of thousands of workers died while building the Qin and Han wall sections. The history of the China-wall-building has fascinated the world for centuries. We hiked up to the top and were informed about the purpose of constructing, and later defending, the wall. Upon successfully completing the hike and the course we received a graduation certificate with our names on it stating we had successfully completed the China Wall Course, including the hike to the top. The experience was unforgettable.

COLOSSEUM (626)

Sometime ago we attended a financial business meeting in Rome and were offered an outing to the colosseum on our free day. We went and were warned about the gypsy children who are skilled rip off artists; they were all over the place and before you realize it, they have your wallet. Being warned we put our passport and credit cards in the socks and wore long pants. My friend Mike yelled, that girl got my wallet, but his wife had seen it, was fast and chased the gypsy girl wrestled her to the ground sat on her, ripped her blouse open and said I have 3 wallets here who of you is missing one? She recovered all in fast order everyone got theirs back, thanks to Mike's wife. Then we hired a guide and toured the structure. The Colosseum construction began under Emperor Vespasian (69-79 AD) and was completed in 80 AD. It was built of travertine limestone, tuff volcanic rock, and brick faced concrete. It could hold an estimated 50,000 to 80,000 spectators at various times in history, with an average audience of some 65,000; it was used for gladiator contests, and public spectacles including animal hunts, executions, sports, and drama. The name Colosseum is believed to be derived from a colossal statue of Nero, who (with support of the Praetorian Guard and the Senate), became the fifth Roman emperor. He was not known to be an angel; in his early years he was advised and guided by his mother, but when he felt the power of being an emperor, he had his mom murdered in a family power struggle and was implicated in the death of his wife Claudia Octavia so he could marry Poppaea Sabina who was married to his stepbrother, therefore he was also eliminated. His contributions to the Empire were: construction of amphitheaters, athletic games, and contests. Over time the statue of Nero was moved to a nearby location. In the year 217 AD the Colosseum was seriously damaged by a major fire caused by lightening, it destroyed the upper levels of the wooden structure, which was not fully repaired till many years later. It has undergone several use changes. In the 6th century a small chapel was built in to the amphitheater with no particular religious significance. Then the arena was converted into a cemetery. In the 12th century the Frangipani family took it over, fortified it, and used it as their castle. In the 14th century the Pope moved out of Rome to Avignon, in France, resulting in the fact that the population of Rome declined and the Colosseum fell in to disrepair. Over the centuries it has been substantially ruined by earthquakes, and stone robbers. It is still a renowned symbol of Imperial Rome and has been listed as one of the 7 Wonders of the World; it is today one of Rome's most popular tourist attractions. The Pope leads torchlight "*Way of the Cross*" procession on Good Friday around the Colosseum, and it's depicted on the Italian 5 cent Euro coin.

EMPEROR PENGUIN (627)

The emperor penguin is the tallest and heaviest of all living penguin species; it is endemic to Antarctica; the male and female are similar in size and may reach 100 cm (39 in) in length and weigh 22 to 45 kg (49 to 99 lb). Like all penguins, they do not fly, but can remain submerged in that freezing water for 20 minutes and dive to a debt of 535 m (1755 ft). They breed during the Antarctic winter and walk over the ice for 50–120 km (31-75 mi) to breeding colonies which may contain up to several thousand penguins, then walk back. The lifespan of the penguin is typically 20 years, although some have lived up to 50. Their habitat is the South Pole. Males and females are about the same size and coloration. The adult has deep black dorsal feathers, covering the head, chin, throat, back, dorsal part of the flippers and tail. The black plumage is sharply delineated from the light-colored plumage elsewhere. In juveniles, the auricular patches, chin and throat are white while its bill is black. The predators of the emperor include birds and aquatic mammals, such as Southern giant petrels, that are the predominant land predator of chicks, responsible for over one-third of chick deaths in some colonies. Occasionally a parent may attempt to defend its chick from attack, although it may be more passive if the chick is weak or sickly. The orcas and the leopard-seal are the known predators to attack healthy adult emperor penguins. Courtship is generally about March or April when the temperature can be as low as 40 below zero. A lone male gives an ecstatic display, where it stands still and places its head on the chest giving a courtship call for 1–2 seconds, it then moves around the colony and repeats the call. One a connection is made the male and female stand face to face with one extending its neck up and the other mirroring it; they both hold that posture for several minutes. Once decided, they waddle around the colony with the female usually following the male; before copulation they bow deeply to each other. Contrary to popular belief, emperor penguins do _not_ mate for life; they are serially monogamous having only one mate each year and remain faithful to that mate throughout the year. The female lays a single egg which is incubated by the male for about two months while the female returns to the sea to feed, if one of then drops the egg and it cracks during the transfer process the baby dies it cannot live in subfreezing temperatures, then both parents waddle back to the water, their relationship has ended and both are single again. If the chick hatches before the mother returns from the sea, the father is able to produce crop milk to sustain the chick 4 to 7 days until the mother returns from fishing; after the chick is born they take turns to baby-sit and watch the chick in the colony.

GREAT BARRIER REEF (628)

The Great Barrier Reef is the world's largest coral reef system off the East Coast of Queensland Australia. It consists of about 344,400 square km (133,000) square miles. It can be seen from outer space and is the world's biggest single structure made by living organisms. It is composed of, and built by billions of tiny organisms know as coral polyps. It supports a wide diversity of life and was selected as a World Heritage site in 1981. CNN labeled it one of the Seven Natural Wonders of the world in 1997. The Queensland National Trust named it a state icon of Queensland in 2006. A large part of it is protected by the Great Barrier Reef Marine Park, which helps to limit the impact of Human use such as fishing and tourism. Other environmental pressures on the reef and its ecosystem include runoff of man made pollutants. According to a study published in October 2012 by the National Academy of Science, the reef has lost more then half its coral cover since 1985, a finding reaffirmed by a 2020 study which found that over half of the reefs coral cover to have been lost between 1995 and 2017. A March 2016 report stated that coral bleaching was more widespread than previously thought seriously affecting ocean temperatures. One publication published an obituary for the reef, although the article was seriously criticized. The Great Barrier Reef Marine Park Act of 1975 stipulates an Outlook Report on the Reefs health pressures and future every five years. The last report was published in 2019. The Australian Institute of Marine Science conducts annual surveys of the Great Barrier

Reef status and the 2022 report shows the greatest recovery in 36 years. It is mainly due to the regrowth of two thirds of the reefs fast growing Aeropora coral, which is the dominant coral there. Eastern Australia experienced in recent years tectonic uplift and Queensland has suffered from volcanic eruptions, some of these became volcanic islands. A previously undiscovered reef of 500 meters tall and 1.5 km wide at the base was found in the northern area in 2020, there are no atolls in the system, and reefs attached to the mainland are rare. Thirty species of cetaceans have been recorded in the Great Barrier Reef including the dwarf Minke Whale, more then 1500 fish species live on the reef; forty nine species of mass spawn with eighty four other fawn species have been observed. Six species of sea turtles come to the reef to breed in the beds of sea grass that is also a fish habitat. Saltwater crocodiles live in mangrove and salt marshes on the coast near the reef. Around 125 species of shark, stingray, skates or chimaeras live on the reef. Giant clam and various cone snails, and more then seven frog species live there. It may well be the world's largest aquarium.

AMAZON RAINFOREST (629)

The Amazon rainforest (aka) Amazon Jungle, or Amazonia, is a moist broadleaf tropical rainforest encompassing 7 million sq km, (2.7 million square miles), located in Brazil (60%), Peru, (13%), Colombia (10%), the remaining 17% divided between, Ecuador, French-Guiana, Venezuela, Guyana, Suriname, and Bolivia, Together these comprise the largest tropical rainforest in the world, with an estimated 390 billion individual trees in about 16,000 species at least 40,000 plants have been identified many of which have medicinal benefits, for that reason the Amazon rainforest has been referred to as the worlds largest medicine cabinet. The bulk of which is still unknown, but here are some that are known: *Quinine* is a muscle relaxant and was the first effective medicine to treat malaria. *Vincristine* and *Vinblastine* are used to treat different types of cancer, with this medicine the chance of surviving childhood leukemia has dramatically increased. There are thousands more many still not discovered. More then 30 million people of 350 different ethnic groups live in the Amazon, subdivided into 9 different national political systems and 3,344 indigenous territories. Indigenous people make up 9% of the total population, and 60 of the groups remain largely isolated. The name Amazon is said to arise from a war Francisco de Orallana fought with Tapuyas and other tribes. The women fought alongside the men. Many tribes were warlike, and more than a third of the males have died from these wars; that is especially so among the Munduruku tribe those expanded along the Tapajos River and its tributaries and were feared by neighboring tribes. In the early 19th century the Munduruku tribes were pacified and subjugated by the Brazilians. During the Amazon rubber boom it is estimated that diseases such as *typhus* and *malaria* brought by immigrants, may have killed up to 40,000 native Amazonians. In 1961, British explorer Richard Mason was killed by an uncontacted Amazon Tribe known as the Panara. Nine countries share the Amazon basin–Even though most of the rainforest is contained within the boarders of Brazil. The Amazon Rainforest has often been referred to as the lungs of the planet, some have alleged that the rainforest produce 20% or more, of the earth's oxygen. There are also some credible reports that have shown an alarming number of wildfires and some scientists have indicated that these fires have consumed more then half of that oxygen. Much is still unknown, but we do know a jungle that size has an overwhelming number of plant and animal species that live there and still need to be discovered.

GRAND CANYON (630)

The Grand Canyon is a steep-sided canyon carved by the Colorado River in Arizona, U.S. The Grand Canyon 446 km (277 miles), some areas are 18 miles wide and are over 1 mile deep. The Canyon and adjacent rim are contained within Grand Canyon National Park the Kaihab National Forest, Grand Canyon-Parashant National Monument, the Hualapai Indian Reservation, the Havasupai Indian Reservation, and the Navajo Nation. President Theodore Roosevelt was a major proponent of the preservation of it and on numerous occasions he came to enjoy the scenery. We can see why. We visited an early morning when the Sun came up and took the scenic walk along the rim in that early morning when the first ryes peek over the horizon these are awe inspiring moments of sheer grandeur. I think it might have been the *Bright Angel Trail* that we hiked, stopping at several viewing posts; it is so inspiring we understood why it was called one of the 7 natural wonders of the world. The Pueblo people who arrived from Spain in 1540 considered the Grand Canyon a holy site known for its visually colorful landscape and overwhelming size. Walking along the rim we must have been there at the right time, people have said they experienced rain but we had only an early morning sun greeting us over the horizon, a near perfect site except for the fact that it was chilly and we were not dressed for the occasion and needed to move on to the east coast and were on limited time to catch our ship to Europe and travel on. However the Grand Canyon may well have been the highlight of the entire trip, to see the grandeur and majesty and the sheer size can not be described here in simple language.

There are many things to do and see, Cruising the Colorado River in a rubber raft, stargazing to see the clarity of the night skies would be an exceptional experience, take a 2 mile hike from the parking lot along the rim, which is what we did; visit the park's souvenir store, but we were there too early in the day, take the village train for 64 mile ride through the Pine forest and meadows, there is a 7 mile hike but we needed to move on. It was an unforgettable experience and regret that we were not able to stay longer. How old is the Grand Canyon? I am not a scientist and my interest is more in the grandeur majesty and beauties of God's Creation rather then consider its age. In that respect I am reminded of my favorite Statesmen Everett Dirksen when Congress discussed the budget. He said: "*a billion here and a billion there, pretty soon you are talking some real money*". When discussing the Grand Canyon scientists talk that way about years. Being among the 6 million visitors, the grandeur we saw 60 years ago is still clearly in the mind.

BIG BEN (631)

Big Ben is the nickname of the Great Clock of Westminster; it uses its Victorian mechanism, having said that there is now an electric motor on standby just to serve as backup. The clock name was often intermingled with the clock tower, but that has now changed. The tower was renamed: The "*Elizabeth Tower*" in 2012 to mark the Diamond Jubilee of Elizabeth II the queen of England at that time. The tower was designed by Augustus Pugin in a neo-Gothic style. When completed in 1859, the clock was the largest and most accurate four-faced striking and chiming clock in the world, the origin of the nickname is open to question, it's possible that Big Ben might have been named after Sir Benjamin Hall, who oversaw the installation, or it may have been heavyweight boxing champion Benjamin Caunt. The tower stands 96 m (316 feet tall, and the climb from ground level to belfry is 334 steps. Its base is square measuring 12 m (40 feet) on each side. Dials on the clock are 6.9 m (40 feet) on each side; all four nations of the UK are represented on the tower shields featuring a *rose* for England, a *thistle* for Scotland, a *shamrock* for Ireland, and a *leek* for Wales. The largest of the tower's five bells weighs 13.5 long tons; it was the largest bell in the United Kingdom for 23 years. The tower is a British cultural icon recognized all over the world it's one of the most prominent symbols of the United Kingdom and Parliamentary Democracy and has been a UNESCO World Heritage Site since 1987. In 1873 a new feature called the Ayrton light was added, it's a lantern sited above the belfry and is lit whenever the House of Commons are in session after dark. It was done so that Queen Victoria could see out of her window at night and know that the Commons were at work. The whole frame is 22.5 feet in diameter making it the third largest in the UK it has 324 pieces of opalescent glass. Originally the dials were backlit using gas lamps, at first only when Parliament was sitting, but have routinely been illuminated from dusk till dawn since 1876. Electric bulbs were installed at the beginning of the 20th century. At the base of each dial is a Latin inscription which means: "_O Lord, keep safe our Queen Victoria the First_". When the clock was completed the frame and hands were Prussian blue, but were painted black in the 1930's to disguise the effects of air pollution. The clocks movement is known for its reliability, construction was entrusted to clockmaker Edward John Dent; after his death in 1853 his stepson Frederick dent took over and completed the work in 1854, however the final touches were done in 1859. Those of us who have seen and heard it, it's unquestionably the work of real professional artists as well as being a superior horologist.

CHICHEN ITZA (632)

Chichen Itza is located 120 miles from the modern-day resort town of Cancun on Mexico's Yucatan Peninsula. The name Chichen Itza is a Mayan language term. They were an ethnic group who had risen to power in the northern part of the Yucatan peninsula, where the city is located. Historic accounts differ as to when Chichen Itza was built and ultimately developed into a center of substantial political and economic power. Some accounts place the establishment of the city around 400 AD, but not all historians agree, some suggested construction started much later, may have been not till the middle of the fifth century. What is not open for debate is that Chichen Itza was a significant center of political and economic activity in the Mayan culture by 600 AD. By then, it was already one of the largest cities in the Mayan world covering nearly two square miles with densely packed residential and commercial, structures all made of stone. Chichen Itza even had its own suburbs, with smaller homes occupying the outskirts of the city; at its height, it's believed that as many as 50,000 people lived there. The population may have been fairly diverse, at least by standards of the time with residents immigrating to the city from beyond the Yucatan, including from present day Central America. Although some have attributed the fall of Mayan civilization to the arrival of Christopher Columbus in 1492, and the European colonialists that followed the famous explorer. Other historians believe that much of the political and economic activity of the city had shifted to Mayapan, who were building a newer community to the south and west of Chechen Itza, by the mid-1200. Some claim Chichen Itza may have been raided and looted at that time, however that may well be an issue open for debate, and depend on which historian has been teaching you, the reality is that none of us were there; (*unless your name is Methuselah*). When the Spanish conquistadors arrived in 1526 there was a thriving community. Long after the Spanish had abandoned the area, Chichen Itza became a significant architectural site in the mid 1800s, it remains so today. Thanks to restoration concerns of the Mexican government, a fair number of important structures of the original city are still there and were saved. Some areas have been leveled to accommodate larger structures. Archeologists have discovered that Mayans liked bright colors on their buildings and have been able to preserve some bright <u>red</u>, <u>green</u> and <u>blue</u> colors of the original stone. It was long rumored that human sacrifice has been practiced there, and some findings seem to confirm that to be so. By the 9th century Chichen Itza had become an important regional area with its rulers controlling much of the central and northern Yucatan Peninsula.

PYRAMIDS (633)

Pyramids have been a part of the Egyptian landscape for centuries and are generally known as burial chambers for the great kings; lets take a look at one of these massive structures, called the Great Pyramid of Giza which is the largest Egyptian pyramid and served as the tomb of Pharaoh Khufu, who ruled during the fourth dynasty of the old kingdom, built in the early 26th century BC, which took about 27 years to build. It is the oldest of the Seven Wonders of the Ancient World as well as the only one that has remained largely intact. It is the most famous monument of the Giza pyramid complex which is part of the UNESCO World Heritage Site at "*Memphis and its Necropolis*". It is situated north of three other pyramids of Giza, although this one has been the world's tallest structure 146.6 meters, (481 feet) for 3,800 years. Over time most of the smooth white limestone casing was removed, which lowered the height to 138.5 meters (454.4 ft). The volume has been given as 2.6 million cubic meters (92 million cubic feet). To build that structure an estimated 2.3 million large blocks, was quarried weighing 6 million tones in total, some of them imported by boat on the Nile. It is beyond question that even by today's standards it's a massive structure. (Some historians have alleged, or insinuated, that structures such as this and others were built by slaves, which may well be so, especially knowing that Egypt has not been opposed to slavery, but we've not been able so substantiate that, therefore we are going to leave it there.) The pyramid temple was standing just east of the Great pyramid but has almost entirely disappeared, only some of the black basalt paving remains; there are only a few remnants of the causeway that remain and the rest will need to wait till the next excavation. Archeologists who have studied pyramids for decades such as Dr Zahi Hawass has overseen much of the restoration of these stone step pyramids near Saqarrah. The step pyramid is significant because it's the first stone building constructed by the Egyptians; it also marked a departure from the traditional burial structure known as a Mastaba, which was a rectangular burial mound with sloping walls and a flat roof. Mastabas were mostly built using mud bricks, but occasionally they were stone. The step formed the base and the rest decreased in size so that the smallest was at the top of the structure. King Snefru made further advancements in pyramid building. Snafu's son, grandson and great grandson would build on his ideas. His son Khufu built what is known today as the Great Pyramid where more then two million tons of stone was used. How the ancient Egyptians accomplished this without a compass remains a mystery as does how the pyramid builders built such massive structures without modern tools or conveniences.

HANGING GARDENS OF BABYLON (634)

The hanging gardens of Babylon were one of the Seven Wonders of the Ancient World listed by Hellenic culture. It was a remarkable feat of engineering with an ascending series of tiered gardens containing a wide variety of trees, shrubs and vines resembling a large green mountain constructed of mud bricks, built in the ancient city of Babylon, near present-day Hillah, Babil province in Iraq. The Hanging Gardens name was derived from the Greek word Kremastos, overhanging, which has a broader meaning than the modern English word "_hanging_" and refers to trees being planted on a raised structure such as a terrace. There are several principal writers one of them Berossus (a Babylonian priest of Murdock), he referred to it quite a few times, but perhaps due to my unfamiliarity of him he would not be my favorite. I prefer Josephus, a more trusted name and know him better. History indicates several versions and here is one: The Hanging Gardens were built alongside a grand palace known as _The Marvel of Mankind_, by the Neo-Babylonian King Nebuchadnezzar II (who ruled between 605 and 562 BC), the story is like this: The king had married Amytis (_a Median wife_), she missed the green hills of her homeland, subsequently the King wanting to please the Queen he retained several Architects to design a garden that would please his wife; should it fail he might wish he had found employment somewhere else. Was it the dream as described in Daniel 4, but there is no reference to hanging gardens there or elsewhere in the Bible, Why not? There is no lack of issues in the Bible that require faith, just think Being thrown in to a den of hungry lions and walk out untouched, or walking in a blazing furnish unschorched by the fire and many more, so why not a Hanging Gardens? Some ancient writers have referred to construction of such a garden, and the Bible speaks of the entire nation of Israel taken in to captivity and if a king can transport an entire population to another country, why is it so hard to build Hanging Gardens? Why are we skeptical? Is it a legend or is it real? <u>Think of this</u>: **1**: The Hanging Gardens are the only one of the Seven Wonders of the World, for which a location has not been definitively established, **2**: there is no mention in the Bible or anywhere else of Nebuchadnezzar's wife Amyitis, although not impossible. **3**: No archeological evidence that has ever surfaced of such a garden, **4**: "<u>Babylon</u>" means "*gate of the gods*" was a coveted name for many Mesopotamian cities, which is it? The Hanging Gardens of Babylon may be a great story, but would fit better in a poetry book.

KEUKENHOF TULIP SHOW (635)

The English translation is kitchen garden, however it is better known as the Garden of Europe, even more fitting would be The World's Flower Garden. It was established in 1949 and opened for the first time to visitors in 1950. It was an immediate success they had 200,000 visitors the first year. Since that time each autumn 40 gardeners plant 7 million bulbs that are donated to the park by over 100 growers. Planting starts in October and ends in December. It operates under a charitable foundation of Count Carel de Graaf van Lynden. The park is situated in the municipality of Lisse which is in the province of South Holland southwest of Amsterdam and easily accessible by bike, car, bus, or train, having always had access to a car we have visited three times, each time it is more beautiful. The Keukenhof Tulip Show is 79 acres. About seven million flower bulbs are planted annually in the park, although it's primarily a tulip show, they feature numerous other flowers including hyacinths, daffodils, carnations, irises, lilies, and roses. On our three personal visits it is as much fun to bring family as we had when we were small children going to a very rare outing. Since having lived overseas we have been back in the country on numerous occasions and at three of such times have visited the park. One time to took my new wife from New Zealand, who always loved the beautiful botanical gardens of New Zealand, and the second time to bring my 82 year old father who loved flowers so much that he said it might have been the highest point in all the 82 years of my entire life, and the third visit was to bring my two married sisters who had also never seen it. The park is only open to the general public for eight weeks from mid March to Mid May with peak time mid April; Since the first year of opening to visitors in 1950 the park now gets a visitors count of about 26,000 per day, which translates into 1.5 million visitors a year; 20% are Dutch, while 40% come from Germany, Belgium and the UK, 10% come from America and about 8% from Japan and China. The fun begins when you drive toward the park and are still 10 to 20 miles away you begin to see the endless flower fields as far as the eye can see. Both sides of the road are just acres upon acres of colorful flowers. It is sight that can never be adequately expressed it is a must see for the eyes to behold. It keeps going and intensifies as you come closer to the park. The homes and farms are all flower farms. The park people are proud of the fact that they receive no government subsidy; ticket sales for the visit and food and beverage licensees support the entire show running about $25 million per year, meaning it's 100% supported by tourism.

MAGNA CARTA (636)

The Magna Carta commonly referred to as <u>The Great Charter of Freedoms.</u> It is a royal charter of rights agreed to by king John of England on 15 June 1215 first drafted by the Archbishop of Canterbury, Cardinal Stephen Langton to make peace between the unpopular king and a group of rebel barons; it promised access to swift justice, protection of church rights from the barons of illegal imprisonment, and limitations on feudal payments to the Crown, to be implemented through a council of 25 barons. Neither side stood behind their commitments, resulting in the fact that the charter was annulled by Pope Innocent III, leading to the First Baron's War. After John's death his young son Henry III reissued the document in 1216, stripped of some of its more radical content in an unsuccessful bid to build support. At the end of the war in 1217, it became a major part of the peace treaty and acquired the name *Magna Carta*, quite different from the smaller charter of the forest. Short of funds, Henry reissued the charter again in 1225 in exchange he promised new taxes. The exercise was repeated in 1297, this time confirming it as part of England's statute law. The charter became part of English political life and was typically renewed by each monarch but as time went by it lost some of its practical significance. During the 16th century there was a new interest in Magna Carta. Lawyers and Historians believed there was an ancient constitution going back to the Anglo-Saxon days that protected individual freedoms, they argued that the Norman Invasion of 1066 had overthrown these rights and Magna Carta was the attempt to restore them. Jurist Sir Edward Coke used Magna Carta extensively in the 17th century arguing against divine rights of kings which two kings, James I and Charles I, attempted to suppress. It was the major issue in the revolution of 1688 and lasted to the 19th century where the colonists wanted it to be a part of the US Constitution which became the supreme law of the US and still forms an important symbol of liberty today often cited by politicians as they campaign and sometimes refer to the 63 clauses of the Magna Carta; but Sir William Blackstone in 1759 argued that the original charter formed a single long unbroken text. The original 1215 charter has been on display at the British Library since 3 Feb 2015 to mark the 800th anniversary of Magna Carta and was referred to as the Great Charter of 10 June 1215 by British leaders at Runnymede, at Staines (the rebel base on the south bank of the River Thames), which was considered a more neutral ground over the royal fortress of Windsor Castle, it offered both sides the security of a rendezvous and place of safety. By June 15 a general agreement was reached. Its 800 years later and most (not all), of the original documents have survived, and are on display at the British Library.

CHERNOBYL DISASTER (637)

The Chernobyl disaster was a nuclear accident on 26 April 1986 when No.4 reactor in the Nuclear Power Plant near the city of Pripyat situated in the north of the Ukrainian SSR Soviet Union, it happen during a safety test to measure the ability of the steam turbine to power the emergency feed water pumps; the completion of the test triggered a reactor shutdown but it had a design flaw which resulted in a meltdown explosion that destroyed the reactor and the building; this released radioactive contaminants getting air-born and were deposited into the USSR and some areas of Europe. (*In Hawaii it was Sunday morning we had just arrived at church and while I was talking to Professor Chuck Hayes he received a call asking for advice Chuck had some expertise in the science of nuclear power*). That morning I was going to be the speaker and Chuck was to lead the singing. We then asked God to help the Ukrainian nuclear engineers and endow them with wise counsel to make the right decision. Such accident is always the first time and those who work there are faced with how to respond to an emergency in which no person has any experience therefore much wisdom is required what should be done. In the nearby city of Pripyat the people were not immediately evacuated the townspeople in the early hours of the morning went about their usual business completely oblivious to what had just happened; but within hours of the explosion dozens of people fell ill with severe headaches, vomiting and uncontrollable fits of coughing. The plant was run by authorities in Moscow and the government of Ukraine did not receive prompt information about the accident. When the fire was extinguished it was assumed that everything would be fine. When officials asked about it the reply was there is nothing to be concerned about some were planning a wedding others were going fishing all were told at first do what u normally do. Then came the 2nd news-bulletin two people had died and 52 got very sick and had been hospitalized _that_ set in motion a prompt evacuation order for all people who lived within a 19 mile radius. 49,000 people were evacuated and moved to an area outside the radius of 30 km (19 mi). Within the plant 2 engineers were killed and several workers were severely burned 237 people were hospitalized of which 134 exhibited symptoms of acute radiation syndrome. Among those hospitalized 28 died within three months. In the following 10 years 14 more workers died, but some may have been unrelated causes. How many died? America differs from Communist governments; America airs all their dirty laundry before the whole world to see the good & the bad; we know it will soon be forgotten. Communist governments go in cover up mode. However the accident has been called: "_the worlds worst-ever nuclear accident_").

VIKING EXPANSION (638)

Viking expansion was the historical movement which led Norse explorers, traders, and warriors to sail most of the North Atlantic, reaching south as far as North Africa, east as far as Russia, and acting as looters, traders, colonists, and mercenaries. To the west Vikings reached as far as North America, Newfoundland and established Norse settlements in Greenland, Iceland, the Faroe Islands, Russia, Ukraine, Great Britain, Ireland and Normandy. There is much debate among historians about what drove the Viking expansion; here are some hypotheses: It was the need to seek out women as was practiced in the 11th century when Viking men would buy or capture foreign women and make them their wives or concubines. The Annals of Ulster states: in 821 Vikings plundered an Irish village and carried off a great number of women into captivity. Another theory is that it was a quest for revenge against continental Europeans for past aggressions against the Vikings and related groups, Charlemagne's campaign to force Saxon pagans to convert to Christianity by killing any who refused baptism. Others believed that the penetration of Christianity into Scandinavia caused serious conflict and divided Norway for almost a century. However the first target of Viking raids was not the Frankish Kingdoms, but Christian monasteries in England. Historian Peter Sawyer reasoned these monasteries were raided because they were centers of wealth and their farms well stocked, they were not raided for any religious reasons. Another theory is that Viking population had exceeded the agricultural potential of their homeland. This may have been true for Western Norway but it is very unlikely that the rest of Scandinavia was experiencing famine. Then there are some scholars who feel that the Viking expansion was driven by a youth bulge effect. Here is why: the eldest son of a family customarily inherited the entire family's estate, younger sons had to seek their fortune by emigrating or engage in raids, girls also got nothing; (a little similar to the philosophy held by the older Japanese generation but there is no indication of any connection). Then there is the possibility that they wanted an expansion of trade routes to acquire and trade silver, a trade previously dominated by the Friesians likely the reason they attempted to destroy the Frisian fleet. In the older texts women are mentioned in the founding of Iceland indicating that Viking explorers were accompanied by women. The name Normandy denotes its Viking origin from Northmannia, _or_ the Land of The Norsemen. The presence in Normandy began with raids into the territory of the Frankish Empire dating back to the 9th century. Not all Vikings were "raiders" some came with families to settle in other parts of Europe and assimilated with the population; many words in European languages come from Scandinavia.

MONACO (639)

The principality of Monaco is a sovereign city-state and microstate of the French Riviera a few kilometers west of Italy on the Mediterranean Sea, (also referred to as Monte Carlo) is one of the smallest countries in the world less then a sq mile (0.78 sq mi), and is home of just under 40,000 people. It is widely recognized as one of the most expensive and wealthiest places in the world. (*We visited on a beautiful sunny day, drove along the coastal road from Genoa along the Mediterranean Sea it was the kind of day you never want to end*). The official language is French although Italian and English are spoken and understood by most residents. After the Vatican-city it is the second smallest country in the world and is the most densely populated sovereign state. Its coastline is 5, 47 km (2.4 mile) and is governed by a constitutional monarchy, with Prince Albert II as head of state. He wields immense political power, although there is a prime minister who is the head of government and consults with the government of France. Key members of the judiciary are detached French magistrates. The House of Grimaldi has ruled Monaco (with brief interruptions) since 1297. Monaco became a member with full voting rights of the United Nations in 1993. Its defense is the responsibility of France. The countries mild climate, beautiful beach, and yacht harbor, In more recent years it acquired a major banking center. Almost half its residents are millionaires with the price of real estate reaching $120,000 per Square meter. The country's economic development got a major boost with the opening of its first casino and a rail connection to Paris. The Casino has greatly contributed to the success of Monaco's economy, but not all is fair weather in Monaco. It has become a global hub of money laundering; *that* and the casino are honey to flies and have already attracted criminal elements from all over the world. We found all these same elements in Las Vegas and Macao wherever major Casinos are a dominant part of the economy. (*Although Stanley Ho of Macao was a friend, we had one thing in common, we both did not gamble*). Monaco is not formally a part of the European Union (EU) but it participates in many of its policies including customs and border controls. Monaco uses the Euro as its sole local currency they joined the Council of Europe in 2004. It is also the host of the Monaco Grand Prix. The principality has a club football team, as Monaco. There is a Center of Marine Research of which I knew Prince Rainier (*husband of Grace Kelly*) had great interest in and was a strong supporter of the Oceanographic Museum, It is labeled as the only marine laboratory, in the United Nations structure and a center of research into marine conservation and is home to the worlds first protected marine habitat.

WAIKIKI (640)

Waikiki is a suburb or neighborhood of Honolulu of the Hawaiian Islands located on Oahu. Waikiki beach is one of the most famous beaches in the world. (*There are three other areas of the world that call their beaches Waikiki, in Tarragona Spain, Lima Peru, and Western Australia, but Hawaii has the best year-round weather*). In the Hawaiian language Waikiki means <u>*Spouting Fresh Water*</u>. In the 1800's Waikiki was a retreat for Hawaiian royalty who enjoyed longboard surfing. Duke Kahanamoku became a well known Waikiki long board surfer; as well as having been competing as a swimmer in the Olympics, where Johnny Weissmuller got the gold and duke brought homer the bronze; he put Waikiki on the map as one of the worlds most notorious surf spots. His 114 pound Koa Wood surf board was 16 ft long. (*The average surfboards of my family made of foam are 5-6 feet long weighing 4-5 pound*). In 1893 Robert Louis Stevenson enjoyed staying in Waikiki. In 1893 Greek American George Lycurgus leased a guesthouse in Waikiki and called it <u>Sans Souci Beach</u>, (a name still often used today). Waikiki beach is one of the most popular beaches in the world but it has a serious erosion problem that began in the late 1800's. According to ocean engineering reports it is because hotels and homes were built too close to the natural shoreline, while seawalls and other structures blocked the natural ebb and flow of sand along the beach. In the early 1900's Waikiki was home to many wetlands which were claimed to harbor disease-carrying mosquitoes; to get rid of the mosquitoes, developers created the Ala Wai Canal, which was first known as the Waikiki Drainage Canal, created by a Hawaiian dredging company run by Walter F. Dillingham who built the canal in seven years 1921-1928. In the 1920's and 1930's sand was imported from Manhattan Beach in California brought to Waikiki by ship or barge, and added to the vanishing beach. By 1950 more than 80 structures including seawalls, groins, piers, storm drains occupied the Waikiki shoreline. Following WW-II restoration efforts occurred every few years 1730 feet (530 m) of beach was replenished at a cost of $2.4 Million. The Biltmore was the first hotel built in 1955 followed by the Sheraton, Princess Ka'iulani, the Hilton Hawaiian Village, Halekulani, Hyatt Regency, Marriott, Moana Surf rider, and the Royal Hawaiian. With more hotels, pristine beaches are essential. The Corps of Engineers drafted an environmental statement, aimed at improving the narrowing and slowly fading shoreline; since 1951 more then 2.8 million cubic feet of sand has been added, but inch by inch the ocean is retrieving it from the most expensive beach in the world taking one foot a year. All the world's engineers have not solved this puzzle.

OCEAN BEACH DISASTER
MAY FIVE 1918 (641)

San Diego police lifesaver was looking for a relaxing Sunday as an estimated 5,000 beach-goers showed up for a day of fun on a Sunday afternoon, balmy conditions almost guaranteed a large crowd at Ocean Beach. At the foot of Newport Ave a fancy new bathhouse was offering free bathing suit rentals as a promotion. Swiftly moving currents, Large crowds, Big surf, and a Lifeguard on the beach, what could possibly go wrong? Lifeguard Chauvaud posted several warning signs advised people to stay in waste deep water near the central area where they could always be seen. He was a savvy lifeguard and swimming instructor who had assisted Police Lifeguard Walt Field for several seasons at Ocean Beach. Navy machinist mate Henry Peter Hanson was stationed at Rockwell Field he was a confident swimmer who often enjoyed the beach. Much of the beach throng that Sunday was largely made up of families, many strong swimmers; many had come several times to Ocean Beach. Author Ruth Varney and Joe Varney strolled along the beach and were people watching. It was a day of families to relax at the beach; many were soldiers from Camp Kearny, the new Army training facility at Miramar established the previous year during World War One, meaning there were a great number of soldiers at the beach with their families frolicking in the sand that beautiful Sunday. In the middle of the afternoon as several large sets rolled through the surf, conditions changed within minutes. Strong and sudden rip currents took the legs out from under surf bathers in even knee deep water. Lifeguard Chauvaud spotted a group of about 20 soldiers heading for the most dangerous area toward Wonderland Point, the North end of Ocean Beach which was the entrance to False Bay and the mouth of the San Diego River. It was long before flood control channel jetties and Mission Bay Park. 75% of surf rescues happen in that area. Chauvaud waved them back but they paid no attention, he shouted at them but they went on after all *we are soldiers*. He blew his whistle but they laughed and plunged in followed by others. They were still in waste deep water when a rip current swept them out beyond their depth. Lifeguard Chauvaud was also knocked of his feet and was grabbed by several flailing bathers and pulled under. Many on the beach hearing the frantic cries for help rushed in the water and were instantly pulled out by a very strong force. Police patrolman Frank Merritt, and part time life saver, grabbed several bystanders to help him pull a lifeline out into the surf. Another dropped his coat and tie, hat and shoes and plunged in after Merit. On that Sunday afternoon 60 were rescued, 40 risked their life, some rescuers were pulled under. Beach warning signs, were not heeded, they are real! *13 people* drowned who ignored the warning signs.

VOTING BY MAIL (642)

About 180 million US adults, (*more than three fourths of the American electorate*), will be eligible to cast their ballots by mail in the next election.

We have voted by absentee (*mail in*) ballot for over 30 years because when I was in business often was traveling on election day, as soon as we received the ballots we voted, signed the envelope, and returned it on the same day. We arrived as foreigners and after waiting the required 5 years, became citizen and have not missed an election in the past 70+ years. Now that we are old and have difficulty getting around, we still want our God-given-right to vote. *When Hitler ruled Europe, my parents still voted but the outcome was always pre-determined.* We have also lived in South America, and make no accusations, but in a fair number of these countries, their election results are questionable. Joseph Stalin might have said it best: "*I do not fear the people who vote, but worry about those who count the ballots.*" In America that issue should be solvable, having said that, to document fraud in mail-in-ballots is not easy to do. According to Heritage Foundation, they examined election in the State of Oregon in 1998 and found 14 cases of attempted mail fraud out of 15.5 million ballots cast, it was the first state to conduct its election exclusively by mail; Washington followed but first made vote by mail optional. The counties embraced the idea of voting by mail claimed it increased voter participation. In 2011 Washington officially went statewide voting by mail; in 2013 Colorado became the third state to adopt statewide vote-by-mail closely followed by Utah. In these states polls continue to show strong support for the vote by mail with little evidence of fraud. In response to the pandemic nearly half the states have now expended to vote by mail; some have provisions requiring voters to cite their reason why they could not vote in person, allowing illness or infirmity, inability to get to the polling site, travel, fear of corona virus was added this year, as an acceptable excuse. Some issues that have created problems are witness requirements for voters unable to complete ballots. Wisconsin reported that 9,000 people requested ballots that were never sent, others said ballots were never received. New Jersey one in ten ballots were rejected for not matching signatures. In Pennsylvania unclear deadline dates disenfranchised tens of thousands of votes, in New York 84,000 ballots were rejected out of 403,000 mail-in-ballots. The US Postal Service is under intense pressure to deliver ballots in a timely manner. As long as there are strong partisan feelings of an entire population there will be problems of derailing a well intended system, therefore we must continually rotate those in charge making sure not one party is in control of the voting process for too long.

SECRETARY OF STATE (643)

A Secretary of State is head of a department with specific functions in the American government, and is a member of the executive branch of the Federal Government, such as the Department of State. He/she is a high ranking member of the president's cabinet, ranks high in the line of presidential succession among Cabinet secretaries. The position was created in 1789 with Thomas Jefferson as first secretary of state, and represented the United States to foreign countries, somewhat analogous to _a minister of foreign affairs_ in most other countries. The Secretary of State is nominated by the president of the United States, following a confirmation hearing before the Senate Committee on Foreign Relations, and confirmed by the United States Senate. The Secretary of State, along with the secretary of the treasury, secretary of defense, and the attorney general, are regarded as the four most crucial Cabinet members due to the importance of their respective departments. The Secretary of State is a level I position in the Executive Schedule and earns the salary prescribed specifically for that position, which is currently in 2023 around $220,000 per year. The Congress of the Confederation established the Department of Foreign Affairs in 1781 and created the office of Secretary of Foreign Affairs. After the Constitution of the United States was ratified, the First US Congress reestablished the department renaming it The Department of State, and created the office of the Secretary of State to lead the department. The stated duties of the Secretary of State are: participate in foreign conferences of US members of Congress; negotiate, interpret, or terminate, treaties; ensures protection of American citizens property and interests in foreign countries; negotiate release of US citizens incarcerated by foreign countries; administrate US Immigration laws abroad; Provide American citizens with information about political, social, and cultural conditions in foreign countries; Advise the president on foreign policy; grants and issues passports to American citizens; advise the president on appointments of US Ambassadors, consuls and diplomatic representatives, including recall of diplomatic personnel when conditions become unsafe; supervise and administer the Dept. of State; communicates conditions about foreign policy and advise Congress on such matters, advice citizens who travel to unfriendly nations; protects, and has custody of, the Great Seal of the US; negotiates hostage releases. Resignation of the president must be presented to the secretary of state. Six past secretaries of state have been elected to the office of President: Jefferson, Madison, Monroe, John Quincy Adams, Van Buren, and Buchanan. Others have tried and lost; for some it has been a consolation prize for failed presidential candidates.

CARIBBEAN (644)

The Caribbean region is named after the Caribs, an ethnic group present in the Antilles and parts of the adjacent South America dating back to the Spanish conquest. I arrived in the Caribbean islands in the late 1950's and lived there 3 years, first in Curacao and later in Aruba. The weather is sub tropical with mild winters along with occasional hurricanes coming through. Living there we took advantage of visiting Venezuela, Trinidad, Barbados and others, for hiking and site-seeing. The Caribbean has many languages, although three are primary: English, Dutch, and Spanish and most locals use a special dialect just for themselves. (*Papiamento is spoken on Aruba, a mixture of Spanish, English, Dutch and some words only known to those who use it.*) There are more than 700 islands in the region. Island arcs delineate the northern and eastern edges of the Caribbean Sea; the Greater Antilles in the north, and lesser Antilles which includes the Leeward Antilles in the east and south. The nearby Lucayan Archipelago, comprising the Turks, Bahamas, and the Caicos islands all are part of the Caribbean despite not bordering the Caribbean Sea. (*Much later we visited the Bahamas but were quite disappointed, perhaps due to the fact that twice we had visited the pristine beauty of Bermuda just outside the Caribbean area, and the Bahamas was not what we were told*). All the islands in the Antilles plus the Lucayan Archipelago form the West Indies, which is often interchanged with the term Caribbean. Surinam, Belize, Guyana, and are often included as part of the Caribbean due to cultural ties. Geopolitically, the islands of the Caribbean are sometimes regarded as a sub region of North America, but should be included in South, or Central America. The Caribbean Islands are organized into 33 political entities including 13 sovereign states, 12 dependencies, <u>one disputed territory:</u> (*Navassa, a small Island, 40 miles from Cuba, primarily a bird sanctuary, while ownership is in dispute between Cuba, US, Haiti, and Jamaica, all of who argue over boundary rights, the birds decided to claim it for themselves and have their babies there, it is as a bird sanctuary undisturbed by humans.*) There are other territories, such as the Netherlands-Antilles composed of five islands all of which were Dutch dependencies and the West Indies Federation are ten English speaking territories, all of which were British dependencies. The Caribbean is mainly a chain of islands surrounding the Caribbean Sea; to the north and is bordered by the Gulf of Mexico, the Straits of Florida and the Northern Atlantic Ocean. The word Caribbean has other uses that are not geographical and political, but have physiographical meaning, such as <u>strong cultural and historical connections to Africa</u>, <u>Slavery</u>, <u>European-Colonization</u>, and the <u>Plantation system</u>.

SING-SING (645)

Sing Sing Correctional Facility was a maximum-security prison operated by the New York State Department of Corrections. The prison employs 900 people, and opened in 1826. That time it was considered a model prison because it turned a profit for the state; one unique feature was absolute silence by the prisoners enforced by whipping and other punishments. It was John Luckey, the prison chaplain, who advised the governor to remove the principal keeper. After that, Luckey created a religious library and Eliza Farnham who was put in charge of the women's ward and the library aimed to teach moral principles; NY Prison Association was inaugurated in 1844 to monitor prison administrations, made up of reformers interested in humane treatment of prisoners. Farnham was instrumental in overturning the *strictly silence* practice and introduced social engagement shifting concern to the future instead of dwelling on past criminal behavior. She included novels of Charles Dickens and other novels in the library, of which the chaplain not approve. It was the first time a prison library included moral teaching from secular literature. In 1914 Thomas Mot Osborne took over as warden, his reputation was prison reforms. Prisoners who had bribed officers and intimidated inmates lost their privileges under Osborne's regime, one of them conspired with powerful political allies to destroy his reputation, even succeeded in getting him indicted on false charges; when Osbourne triumphed in court his return to Sing-Sing was cause for a wild celebration at the prison. In 1919 Lewis Lawes took over as warden and remained there 21 years; he brought many reforms and turned what was referred to as the "_old hellhole_" in to a modern prison with sports teams, educational programs and new methods of disciplines; Lewis retired in 1941 and died six years later. The original name "_Sing-Sing_" was derived from the Sintsink Native American tribe from whom the land was purchased in 1685. In 1970 the prison name was changed to Ossining, but reverted back to Sing-Sing in 1985. It holds 1,700 inmates and housed the electric chair nicknamed "_Old Sparky_" in which 614 men and women were executed until America abolished the death sentence in 1972. High profile executions include Julius and Ethel Rosenberg on 19 June, 1953 for espionage _for_ the Soviet Union on nuclear weapon research; the last person executed at Sing-Sing was Eddie Lee Mays on 15 August 1963. Eventually in 1972 the death penalty was abolished, at least not used again and _Sparky_ was retired. Katherine Vockins founded Rehabilitation in 1966 through art enabling theater professionals provide year round workshops which a professional study found had a positive impact on prisoners; prison reform, college education, and football teams, at Sing-Sing are still unfolding.

THE PRAYER OF KING JEHOSAPHAT (646)

The prayer of King Jehosaphat is recorded here for us in 2 Chronicles 20: the Moabites, Ammonites and some Meunites with their vast armies came to make war on Judah. Gods people had already been harassed by them before and letting them live may be was a mistake, but Moses only made few of them, not too many. Jehosaphat knew that an army of that size could not be defeated unless he had nuclear weapons. So what should this Godly old king do? The atomic bomb had not come out yet, and neither he nor his advisors had any answers that made sense and he knew what would happen therefore, he called for a full congregational meeting and rather then tells the leaders: _y'all_ go in your closet and ask God for help. That would have been the least embarrassing way to do it especially if God did not respond. But instead the king himself stood in their midst and said: "O Lord God of our fathers, are you not the God who is in heaven? You rule over all the kingdoms, in the past you helped Abraham, your friend, and his children we are his descendents and did not steal this land but you gave it to Moses and Aaron and we are still here, and if calamity comes upon us whether the sword of judgment of plague or famine we will stand in your presence before this temple that bears your name and will cry out to you in our distress, and you will hear us and save us. But now these men from Moab, and Mount Seir, whose territory you would not allow Israel to invade when they came from Egypt so they turned away and did not destroy them. Now they have multiplied and are strong and far more numerous then we are, they are coming to drive us out. We have no power, and we do not know what to do. There is no way we could defeat them. But...our eyes are upon u. Just incase he would be ridiculed he did that in his private closet? _NO!_ He prayed this before all the men of Judah who with their wives and children stood there before the Lord. That took courage and much faith. This was very real the enemies are all here and we have no power against them, they must have remembered we have settled here in this land and we let them live and multiply, and now they come for revenge, and Jehosaphat may be their king but he <u>publicly confesses before all the people</u>: we do not know what to do. It would be the devil's intention that we flee in fear. Perhaps it's not the Ammonites and the Moabites and the Meunites that are crossing our borders, but could it be that King Jehosaphat stood before his people for such a time as this, and has the time come for us to look at <u>the gospel of Pogo</u> which may give us a deeper truth than we give credit to it, quoting from his book: "_<u>We found the enemy and it's us.</u>_"

QUEEN OF SHEBA (647)

The Queen of Sheba came to Jerusalem to visit King Solomon in order to test him with hard questions as it is recorded in the Biblical account of 2 Chronicles 9. She came with a great caravan with camels carrying spices, large quantities of gold and precious stones. Solomon answered all her questions; nothing was too hard for him to explain to her all that was on her mind. When she saw the Wisdom of Solomon, and the palace he had built, the food on his table, the seating of his officials, the attending servants in their robes, the cup-bearers, the burnt offerings he made at the temple of the Lord, she was overwhelmed and said to the king. The report I heard in my country about your achievements and your wisdom is true; but I did not believe it until I came and saw with my own eyes. Not even half of the greatness of your wisdom was told me; you have far exceeded the reports I heard about you. How happy your officials must be who continually stand before you and hear your wisdom. Praise be to the Lord your God who has delighted in you and placed you on His throne as king and rule for the Lord your God. Because of the love of your God for Israel and his desire to uphold them forever, he has made you king over them to maintain justice and righteousness. Then she gave the king 120 talents of gold, large quantities of spices and precious stones. There had never been such spices as those the queen of Sheba gave to King Solomon. King Solomon gave the queen all she desired and asked for; he gave her more than she had brought to him. Then she left and returned with her retinue to her own country. Historians have identified Sheba with South Arabian kingdom of Saba which in present day terms would be Yemen and Ethiopia. There is no shortage of scholars who are "_wiser_" than the Biblical writers for that reason many scholars dispute the existence of the Queen of Sheba; however: Sheba was quite well known in the classical world and in that world the country was called Arabia Felix. There is other reference to Sheba in Psalm 72, (_but that psalm was written by Solomon, meaning it would not help the skeptics_). One thing is apparently quite well accepted and that is of the wisdom of King Solomon which was well known throughout the then known world. The temple that he had built, the story about suggesting to cut a baby in half, just to get to the truth, was the type of news that had spread throughout the entire world even without New York Times and CNN. The Gospels of Matthew and Luke refer to the Queen of the South who came to enquire about Solomon's wisdom. It is my opinion _if_ the Queen of Sheba is to be questioned we would need to question the entire Bible, then where do you end; therefore we believe the entire Bible is the Word of the living God and is not fallible, and that includes the queen of Sheba.

REICH'S-AUTOBAHN (648)
(GERMAN FREEWAYS)

During the 1930's some mentioned controlled-access highways; but people could not imagine the concept, especially when at that time there were few automobiles. All of Europe was pretty much a bike world. The Weimar Republic had constructed a few of such roads, but it was received with mixed emotion and people began to look at such highways a little puzzled at first; in the mid thirties there was virtually no traffic, so what could be the motive. This upcoming young soldier (*born in Austria*) called Hitler, wanted more of these roads, especially when the Nazis gained more control of Europe people embraced the idea with skepticism. Was it his ego? Hermann Goering Minister of defense for the Reich liked it too. Hitler was claiming more and more power the early auto-bans were even named "*Straben Adolf Hitler's*" meaning Adolf Hitler's roads. He performed the first ceremonial shoveling of dirt on 23 Sept. 1933 at Frankfurt; after that work was done simultaneously at multiple sites throughout the Reich; the first finished stretch was the road from Frankfurt to Darmstadt opened on 19 May 1935 and the first 1,000 km (620 mi) were completed 23 Sept. 1936. Then in conjunction with the annexation of Austria, a second sod-breaking ceremony took place, this time at Salzburg on 7 April, 1938; that road was 3800 km (2.300 mi) completed in 1941 which was at the beginning of World War II. When the Nazis came to power in

Europe Hitler presented it as a necessity pointing out railroads was an era of the past. In the mid 1930's autobahn construction work was operating at 22 locations, governed by 9 regions Hitler had two controlled-access highways built with unemployed labor; Konrad Adenauer also embraced the idea and constructed a ring-road around Cologne, followed by other cities dong the same. We took the children and stayed a week at Munich and loved that ring road around the city; during the day we went site seeing in Bavaria and were always happy to get on the ring-road not having to travel through the inner city going back to our hotel. With increased population more such highways became the primary method of traveling from one city to another. General Eisenhower like the idea and called them freeways and thought America needed that. Hermann Goering also began to like the idea when 15,000 workers were engaged in building high speed highways. We traveled most of these European highways, and are fascinated by how little repair takes place. An engineer told me the quality of the material used in surfacing the European highways is superior to what America is using they get more rain but have no potholes. We saw no maintenance workers only new construction projects. Europe seems to get more rain, but have better quality drainage.

PRO LIFE ISSUE REVISITED (649)

In high school in the Philippines Cathy experienced and lived through a devastating earthquake that heavily damaged her school. She watched her classmates being rescued from the rubble, that's when she decided on a career to help others. She served for a year in the Philippine Natl. Red Cross and became a nurse, then moved to New York and was hired as operating room nurse in a NY Hospital. In her job interview she explained that her Catholic faith guided her in the preservation of human life and made it clear that she could not ever assist in abortions, and was committed to healing not killing of human life. Hospital officials assured her that the hospital had a written policy allowing employees to decline to participate in such procedures; she completed a form allowing her to decline in abortion procedures. But promises made five years after Cathy was hired were forgotten; she received a call that she needed to come and assist on a dilation and curettage surgery which is used for mothers who suffer a miscarriage. Cathy went in to the surgery room and prepared it for the patient. She saw a cart arrive with instruments and knew this was not a miscarriage but preparations were being made for an abortion. She called the resident assigned to the case who informed her that the surgery was an abortion on a live 22 week-old baby. The mother had been diagnosed with a condition Cathy had treated many times without killing the baby, meaning the abortion was not needed. She called her supervisor and consistent with her longstanding objection she could not participate in the abortion. The supervisor then called her supervisor and said that Cathy _must_ participate in the abortion it was needed to save the mothers life. Cathy knew from her medical experience that was not true. In addition to the fact that the surgery was characterized a "_Category II_" meaning it had to take place within 6 hours, which would give the hospital enough time to find another nurse. But the officials refused. Cathy was advised if you do not help in the abortion you will be charged with "_Insubordination and patient abandonment_," which would threaten her career and livelihood. She tearfully pleaded to be excused from participating in the abortion but they would not budge and forced her to help while the baby was being dismembered. She filed a grievance report with her union but her supervisors refused to meet with her. She was told if you want to continue to work here you must participate in abortions if they are designated emergencies. She went to ADF and was supplied with free legal counsel who filed a lawsuit, and asked the HHS to investigate the hospital practice. The result was the hospital needs to revise its policy. What about Cathy? She has nightmares about what she was forced to witness. This is not the America I got to know in the 1950's.

TOWER OF PISA (650)

The tower of Pisa is a free standing bell tower of Pisa Cathedral in Italy and is world renown for its nearly four degree lean, which is the result of an unstable foundation. The height is 55 meter (183 feet) on the low side and 56 Meter (186 feet) on the high side. It has 296 or 294 steps depending what side you walk up. The tower began to lean during construction in the 12th century; there is some controversy about the identity of the architect. For many years it was attributed to Guglielmo and Bonanno Pisano a well known 12th century resident-artist. Pisano left Pisa in 1185 for Sicily but came back to die. A 2001 study seems to indicate Diotisalvi was the original architect due to other work he did at that time as well as being credited for the bell tower of San Nicola and the Baptistery, both in Pisa. Construction of the tower occurred in three stages over 199 years. On 5 January 1172, Donna Berta di Bernardo, a widow and resident of the house of dell'Opera di Santa Maria, bequeathed sixty soldi to the Opera Campanilis petrarum Sancte Marie. The sum was then used toward the purchase of a few stones which still form the base of the bell tower. On 9 August 1173, the foundations of the tower were laid. Work on the ground floor of the white marble campanile began 14 August of the same year during a period of military success and prosperity. The ground floor is a blind arcade. The tower began to sink after construction of the second floor in 1178 due to weak unstable subsoil, a design that was flawed from the beginning; construction was halted for almost

100 year. Beginning on 27 December 1233 Benenato continued the construction project. In 1264 master builder Giovanni di Simone and 23 workers went to the mountains to cut marble. The cut stones were given to Rainaldo Speziale in 1272 construction resumed under Di Simone. In an effort to compensate for the tilt the engineers built upper floors with one side taller than the other. Because of this the tower is curved. In 1284 construction was halted when Pisans were defeated by the Genoese in the battle of Meloria. The seventh floor was completed in 1319, and the bell chamber was added in 1372 by Tommaso di Andrea Pisano who harmonized the Gothic elements of the belfry. There are seven bells; one for each note of the musical major scale, the largest was installed in 1655. During World War II, the allies suspected that the Germans were using the tower as an observation post, Leon Weckstein was sent to confirm the presence of German troops in the tower. He was impressed by the beauty of the cathedral and the tower, thus refrained from ordering an artillery strike thereby sparing it from destruction. All effort to restore the tower to a vertical position has failed. In 1993 a counterweight of 870 tonnes was installed. Engineers have stated the tower is stable for another 300 years.

GLADIATORS (651)

A gladiator swordsman was an armed combatant who entertained audiences in the Roman Republic in violent confrontations with other gladiators, wild animals, or condemned criminals. Although there were some volunteers who risked their lives, their legal and social standing by appearing in the arena. Most were despised slaves, schooled under harsh conditions or were sentenced to death meaning when they fought in the arena it might be the only opportunity to live a little longer. Their value as entertainers was commemorated primarily in the Roman world; early literature sources do not agree on the origins of gladiator games therefore we are leaving that open for debate. The games may have lasted for about a thousand years reaching their peak between the 1st century BC and the 2nd century AD. Christians disapproved of the games because of the idolatrous pagan rituals and there was question about the fact that one of the two gladiators often (not always) died which was what the blood thirsty crowd came to see. If the fight was with a wild beast sometimes the beast was victorious, especially if the gladiator was a child. As a rule gladiators were men, but some historians have denoted that in 66 AD Nero used Ethiopian women, and even children, as gladiators to impress King Tiridates I of Armenia. Some Romans found it a novel idea of entertaining visitors in the arena with female gladiators fighting wild boars in arena with spear in hand and breasts exposed although some women would fight from a cart or chariot; female combatants received the same training as their male counterparts. Some regarded gladiators of any type, male or female, a result of corrupt Roman appetites and morals; the last female gladiator fight may have been in about 200 AD. Caligula, Titus, Hadrian and quite a few others are believed to have performed in the arena. Claudius (Characterized by historians as morbidly cruel), fought a whale trapped in the harbor in front of spectators all of whom virtually unanimously disapproved of such performances. There were many gladiator performances that were bloodless sports. In general bloody spectacles do not please the masses. In 365 Valentinian-I threatened to fine a judge who sentenced Christians to the arena. In 393 Theodosius-I adopted Nicene Christianity as the state religion of the Roman Empire and banned pagan festivals. Honorius (395-423) legally ended gladiator games in 399 and again in 404 at least in the Western Roman Empire. Valentinian-III (425-455) repeated the ban. By the year 536-and-beyond interest in gladiator contests had waned throughout the Roman world. In the Byzantine Empire, theatrical shows and chariot races continued to attract crowds who had no apatite for gladiator fights.

ABOUT THE AUTHOR

Terry Bosgra spent his childhood in the Netherlands it was in the 1940's during the time that Hitler was devastating Europe. Amsterdam was considered the Jewish capital of all of Europe; when it became known that the Gestapo was looking for Jews, they instinctively knew what may be coming, was not good. Hitler had a deep hatred for Jews, and used the Wearmacht to spread his poison throughout the troops, who were willing and eager to carry out his malevolent orders. The handwriting was on the wall when 1000 concentration camps were established, fearing the worst, Jewish parents sent their children outside the city to safety. Danger was everywhere but the country was slightly better. The Dutch people were mostly Christian and were quite willing to take in these children, keeping them out of the clutches of rooming soldiers who occupied Holland and most of Europe at that time. Terry's family of 7 children lived further north and many surrounding families opened up their homes to house some of these children. In order for them to assimilate, children's names such as Moses, Abraham or Samson were changed to Piet, Jan. Dirk others. The family was very poor the future did not look promising, therefore when he reached age 17 he had two options; get drafted in the army or volunteer in the Marine Corps; he chose the latter. Terry was eager to go to the war-zone in Korea, during the 1950's but the conflict was winding down, and the Marines were held back and parked in South America, Terry was sent to a Marine base in the Caribbean.

After completing his required 3 years of military commitment he went back to Europe and applied to immigrate to America but there was a seven year waitlist, and the line was long. He then chose a different direction and moved to New Zealand. There he met Pamela, got married and both of them moved to California. After 3 years they returned to New Zealand but from there went back to the US and this time settled in Hawaii. It was Terry's goal to be an airline pilot; he got licensed to fly but was not able to secure a position and started a financial company. It was a success and after 45 years he sold the company, and worked with his friend Hal in Switzerland doing humanitarian relief work in the Middle East and Africa. Then Hal died and in order to keep the brain active Terry began writing books. One of the seven books is his own biography which is still in process.

BOOK FIVE (ALPHABETICAL)

(Issues and event that made a difference)

www.ingramcontent.com/pod-product-compliance
Lightning Source LLC
Chambersburg PA
CBHW020434130626
46549CB00001B/137